Advance Praise for *Stages of Blue*

"My past will always haunt me sometimes," writes Kayla Jeswald, "Even after all those years, those markings still cover my body to remind me of the struggle it went through." Jeswald's *Stages of Blue* is a courageous book that leads her readers through the author's mental health journey from the lowest points of turmoil to "the road to redemption." Jeswald's fearless voice carries throughout the book as she bravely eviscerates her past to bring herself and her readers to where "hope and light" await.

—Molly Fuller, author of *For Girls Forged by Lightning: Prose & Other Poems*

"In *Stages of Blue*, Kayla Jeswald navigates the depths of grief, love, and sorrow. A remarkable debut."

—Christopher Barzak, author of *Wonders of the Invisible World*

Kayla Jeswald's Stages of Blue is an honest, bold, and sincere book of creative nonfiction that speaks to and for those who have encountered anxiety, depression, bi-polar disorder, self-identity, and mental health concerns. Her selection of a mix of genres—essays, memoir, narrative, anecdote, and poetry—not only provides an array of access for interested readers, but informs them of the complexity of the issues at the heart of the book. "I've lost my younger years to depression," she writes, "and I don't want to lose the better years of my life to it." Kayla Jeswald's book of strength and growth unlocks doors for herself and for anyone experiencing these same issues, or for educating concerned family or friends. I highly recommend Stages of Blue.

—Robert Miltner, author of *Hotel Utopia and Orpheus & Echo*

Stages of Blue describes the search for self amid depression and doubt in painful, at times harrowing, detail. Ultimately, though, the book is a testimony to the value of continued struggle, to the importance of not giving in despite grave obstacles, and to the hope and understanding that wait at the end if we persist. This is a courageous book to have written.

—Steven Reese, author of *Excentrica: Notes on the Text*

Stages of Blue

Kayla Jeswald

STAGES OF BLUE
Copyright © 2020 Kayla Jeswald
All Rights Reserved
Published by Unsolicited Press
Printed in the United States of America.
First Edition.

No part of this book may be used or reproduced in any manner whatsoever without written permission except in the case of brief quotations embodied in critical articles or reviews.

Attention schools and businesses: for discounted copies on large orders, please contact the publisher directly.

For information contact:
Unsolicited Press
Portland, Oregon
www.unsolicitedpress.com
orders@unsolicitedpress.com
619-354-8005

Cover Design: Kathryn Gerhardt
Editor: S.R. Stewart
ISBN: 978-1-950730-36-0

Author's Note

This collection is about my life and my struggles with mental illness over the years. I was diagnosed with depression at the age of 15 and lost myself in the disease. At the age of 27, I started experiencing anxiety and was also diagnosed with Bipolar II Disorder, which deals with the more depressive state. I have experienced highs and lows throughout the years as well. I wanted to write this collection to help people better understand mental illness and how it can affect someone. I have damaged relationships over the years due to my illness. I have also pushed people away. This collection deals with a lot of the darkness that I have experienced but also talks about the hope I have received this past year from life finally getting better. There are some extreme cases and situations that I talk about in this collection so please be advised. The names of doctors and loved ones mentioned have been changed to secure their privacy.

Contents

Light Eyes	11
Have You Seen Me?	14
When the Monster Took Over	37
The Right to Panic	46
My Backwards Beer Goggles	63
Undisclosed Information	66
Mush	68
Lack of Sleep (Pattern)	71
A Low Blow to Doubt	75
Brain on Fire	79
Well I'm Not PMS-ing	82
Unfortunate Events	84
Cellulite: My Life Story Told in Braille	89
Banged Up	91
Keep Calm and…	93
The Disappearing Act	95
Black Heart	102
Undisclosed Information Part 2	105
What is Anxiety?	106
Barely Breathing	107
Not a Junkie, Just Desperate	110

Drummer on Speed	112
Nix the Tics	114
Living with the Sahara	116
Constant Discomfort	118
Disturbance in the System	120
The Attack on Myself	122
A Viewing of Jekyll and Hyde	125
Dissecting Depression: Look at it For What it Really is	139
Sunny Disposition	145
Dancing with Depression: A Five Part Movement	147
Bittersweet Goodbye	154
The Road to Redemption	156
About the Author	159
About the Press	160

To my loving and supportive parents— I am sorry for pushing you away over the years. Thank you for being patient with me in my times of need. I know I have screwed up, and I am trying to make up for it now and be better. Thank you for your undying love and support. I would be lost without you both.

To my family, especially my Aunt Margie— I am grateful and blessed to have you all in my life. You have helped me get through some tough times. You were there for me when the crying and anxiety wouldn't stop. You saw me at my darkest moments and still decided to love me unconditionally. I am so thankful and lucky to have you.

To my boyfriend, Dan— Thank you for always checking in on me and trying to understand what goes on with me. Your patience and kindness have been much appreciated. I would be lost without you. Thank you for sticking by my side in these tough times the last couple of years. It has meant so much, and I am lucky to be in a relationship where someone doesn't give up on me or makes me feel bad for dealing with my struggles.

To my friends— I am sorry for being distant over the years, but you seem to be understanding of that. You always ask how I'm doing, and you want to know about my mental illness and if it is under control. I appreciate you always being there for me even when we are miles apart. I love you all.

To my psychiatrist and therapist— Thank you for talking me through my struggles and helping me work on myself. Thank you for listening to me when sometimes others didn't. I appreciate your help and guidance over the years. I am lucky to have found such wonderful people as yourselves.

Light Eyes

They say the eyes are the windows into the soul. They say that if someone really stares deep enough and long enough, they can really see who you are inside. But what if your windows are dirty and covered in shit? You try to whisper your breath and wipe away the fog, but nothing happens. You try to rub away the gunk and crusty pieces stuck in your eyes…or windows…or whatever the fuck you want to call them, but your vision still isn't clear. Maybe this is why no one can really see my soul or who I am. Maybe if my eyes could decide on a color for longer than a day, people could really see me.

I was born with natural baby blues. Most babies are born with cobalt colored eyes but not me. From what my parents tell me, my eyes were the color of the Maldives water; they were crystal clear at first glance, but the deeper you travel, the darker they become. People always comment on my eyes. They tell me how beautiful they think they are or how envious they are of them. I'll admit it. I like the way they light up when my dark brushes against my pale skin. I think I was meant to have blue eyes; I just wish people could see what goes on inside them. They don't see the way they change from their cerulean glow to foggy ash when it begins to rain outside. They don't see the secret meteor shower happening around my iris; tiny white speckles fall like rain drops all around my pupil. The changes outside call to me. They are me, and I am them, but no one has witnessed this yet.

They think the girl with blue eyes is happy, is calm, and is a nice girl. But they don't see the way my sparkling sapphires turn to the color of damp seaweed when my heart and mind have had enough. Very few people have seen my swamp eyes; the eyes that appear after the world has taken its toll on me. I feel so connected to this Earth, to this world, and to the things we cannot see or prove. It eats away at me on a constant basis...but you'll never see that. I'll only show you my baby blues.

Maybe the reason people can't peer through my windows and see my soul is because I don't want them to. I don't have the ability to control my shifting palette, but I do have the ability to hide it. I don't want people to see the real reason for my blue eyes; I just want them to admire them. For I think if they saw the real baby blues, their whole outlook of me would be forever changed.

Why would I want someone to see that the real reason I have dazzling blues? Only to find the awe of them is a lie. They hide the real blue that lives inside me. They are the color of a starless sky that haunts me throughout the day.

My eyes grew darker fifteen years ago when I was just entering high school. The doctors told me that what I was experiencing was a mix of depression, bipolar, and anxiety. How ironic was it to worry about everything and nothing all in one thought? Once again, I became the walking contradiction. It has been fifteen years now, and sad to say, I'm surprised I'm still here. There were moments where I thought I wouldn't make it to the next hour.

Tell me; are you still envious of the girl with dazzling eyes?

Really? Still?

…

Yeah, I didn't think so.

I knew the charm would eventually wear off my baby blues.

STAGES OF BLUE

Have You Seen Me?

My name is Kayla, and I lost myself fifteen years ago.

It came without a warning. One minute I was fine, normal even; the next moment, I was gone. The girl that looked back at me in the mirror was now someone I didn't even recognize. Her face looked like mine in the shimmering glass, but the etched marks engraved around her mouth were not something that I was familiar with.

I know I'm still in there somewhere, but I can't seem to find me. Do you see me?

I seem to ask myself that question a lot. It's hard enough being a teenager and trying to figure out who I am, but when depression interrupts that, it all goes to shit. I've been completely lost within myself for what has seemed like forever. I still look the same. My smile is still the same when it does make an appearance. I haven't recognized myself in a handful of years, and at this rate, I'm not sure I ever will.

The light blue eyes that everyone admired have now shadowed my face in darkness. What was happening to me? I knew it had to do with him. I remember the night he died, all too well in fact. It has already been fifteen years, but ever since that night, I knew a part of me died with him.

I know I'm still in there somewhere, but I can't seem to find me. Do you see me?

I regret everything. I hate the fact that he was dying while I was laying on some beach with my parents. They wanted to take me on a family trip before I entered my first year of high school. I knew it wasn't the right time though. I told him that I loved him before we left. I told Grandma to keep an eye on him and to call us if his health changed.

On the second night of our vacation, I had a dream. I was standing in the back of a crowded room. I didn't know where I was at first, but then I saw everyone crying and realized I was standing at a funeral. The crying reverberated in my ears. It was loud enough to make anyone go insane. Hands began pushing me through the crowd. I could feel my feet skidding across the floor, trying to resist. I got to the front of the room, and there he was lying perfectly still in the casket. My grandfather. My hero. My everything. I woke up with beads of sweat dripping down the side of my forehead. I knew this tornado was just winding up and would hit home very soon.

STAGES OF BLUE

My grandpa, besides my father, was always someone I looked up to. He served our country in the time of war, he protected people as a security guard for a living, and when he retired, his next big job was to keep me laughing (which he always did). I think people always got the wrong idea about him. He was a pretty big guy, wide like a linebacker. His tummy, full of Italian and Hungarian food, always hung a little too far over his belt. The few salt and pepper strands of hair he did have left were combed neatly towards the left side of his head, and his small coke bottle glasses perfectly emphasized his large dark pupils. He always had a straight-laced face, but when he smiled, boy did it light up the room. By the looks of him, you never would have thought he was a giant, cuddly teddy-bear-of-a-man. I try to remember those memories the most.

He always had a deep cough though. I first noticed it when I was little. I thought it was from all the years of smoking, which I guess a part of it was. I remember patting him on the back when I would sit in his lap, trying to burp the coughs out of him like a baby.

It wasn't until I got older that I realized why he was always wheezing. Emphysema. I thought the huffing and puffing after climbing the steps was just because of old age or his gut, but it was this monster slowly cutting off his airway. He was an avid smoker. I have vivid images of clouds of smoke dancing around my head when I was little. Who knew that smoking and working in a factory would be a deadly combination?

The doctor's put him on a portable oxygen tank during his last year on Earth. If it wasn't enough the man could hardly catch his breath, now he had this little tank on wheels haunting his every step. It was a constant reminder that things were getting worse. I knew he wasn't going to make it much longer. He kept saying how he wanted to die, how he didn't want to live his life like this. He kept saying that he was ready to let go, but I wasn't. Grandma wasn't. Dad wasn't.

It's hard not to let the memory of the last time I saw him haunt me. I think it is something that will eat away at me the rest of my life. I try to shake it free, but in the middle of the night, it lurks in the dark corners of my brain and awakens my nightmares.

#

The night it happened

Gray and lifeless. That is the last image I have of him in my head. The paramedics carried his limp body to the ambulance right before my eyes. I knew he was going to die that morning, but I at least thought I would get to say goodbye.

I had told Mom to call my grandparent's house to make sure he was okay, but she wouldn't listen. Maybe if she had called, I could have been there to see him take one more breath. But that's not what happened. The night dragged on, and I was wide awake.

I paced my room for hours in the middle of the night. My gut told me that something was wrong. I knew it was him. Our bond was beyond words; it was feelings and emotions, and right now I was feeling that he was in serious trouble. I knocked on Mom and Dad's door repeatedly, telling them to call him; they thought I was crazy.

"It's the middle of the night, Kayla. Go back to bed. Everything is okay," Mom said in a muffled, half asleep voice.

"But, Mom, you need to call Grandma's house!" I said frantically. "Something is wrong!" No response, just her snores echoed in the room.

I was so frustrated. I couldn't sleep knowing that he was in pain, and if my eyes did close, I only saw him. The shock would wake me even more abruptly.

I forced myself to get back in bed, protected by some awful neon comforter that I picked out for my birthday. Thank God I don't have the taste of a fourteen-year-old girl anymore. The fetal position was my first idea; maybe it would comfort me, but instead I ended up on my back, staring wide-eyed at my ceiling. *Why weren't they listening to me? Did they not love him as much as I loved him? I could try and save him. I could comfort him like all those times he was there for me.* A million things crept through my mind. I finally decided to squeeze my eyes shut and force myself to be calm. A sound stopped that from happening. It was usually a charming noise to hear, but now it was an echoing sound that made me panic.

The phone rang a little after four in the morning, and the pit in my stomach sank deeper.

"Mike! Kayla! Get up! Grandma says Grandpa collapsed in the kitchen and isn't moving! Let's go!" I've never seen my parents so startled before. Everyone jumped out of bed, threw shoes on, and dashed to the car. Even though Grandma only lived a few minutes down the street, it seemed like it took forever to get to him.

None of us were prepared for what we were about to see. I mean, how could you be? How could you be ready to lose a parent and grandparent? I'd never seen my dad so alert. He was staring blankly at the windshield, but his eyes were piercing. It felt like the glass was going to shatter. We arrived at the house and pulled into the grass on the side of the garage.ABlghts danced across the front of the house like tiny fireworks of red and white being shot off.

Two ambulances and a mob of paramedics swarmed the house. Their house was a big two-story home, painted a faint pink color with white shutters. A quaint mailbox with their names etched in the side sat at the bottom of the front porch steps. The lawn looked freshly mowed. The scene was quiet. From the outside, it looked peaceful and welcoming. From the looks of it, you wouldn't think that an old man just took his last breath on the kitchen floor. You probably wouldn't think that my nightmares were created in there.

When entering my grandparents' house, you were stuck in the middle of the house through the front door. You could either walk right downstairs to the basement or climb a flight of stairs to the kitchen and family room. That was where the paramedics were all lined up. I couldn't see him. I saw a fat foot dangling over the top step. It looked a bit stiff with its toenails pointed straight to the ceiling. I tried to sneak in behind the paramedics to climb the steps, but my mother grabbed the back of my coat and told me to wait downstairs. Her and my father would investigate.

I was told to stay in the basement, that I shouldn't be in the way or see such a traumatic thing happen. It was probably the most devastating moment of my life: to know that I had to sit in the cold, dark basement alone, while my hero was possibly dying in the room above my head.

The thought of him dead made tears gush down my face like an endless river. I couldn't control myself. I had to know what was going on. I crept up the steps and slid behind the paramedics that were lined up on the staircase. I could feel the shock settle in as I hit the last step at the top. There he was. His body looked bloated, and all the color was drained from his face. I almost didn't recognize him. I had never seen a dead body before.

I moved out of the way and into the living room so that the paramedics could hurry him to the hospital. But I knew he was already gone. I don't even know why they rushed him out of the house. He wasn't moving, and he wasn't going to. They gave me false hope. Like at any minute, they could blow puffs of air into his lungs, and he would magically prop back up and smile at me. I'd never see him smile again or hear his laugh. That was what haunted me the most.

My father got into the ambulance first. He lifted Grandma's frail body into the ambulance with them as they took off into the night towards the hospital. Mom and I sat on the couch as time slowly passed.

"He is going to be okay, Kayla. Everything is going to be okay," she said. But I knew that she was lying to me. I knew she didn't want to see me hurt. She turned the TV on to try to distract my mind and soothe me. I couldn't look at it. Her arm coiled around me, and her red fingernails grazed my hair. She pulled me into the right side of her chest, and I let my head fall back against her shoulder. Her lips pressed up against my forehead. I noticed sadness in her lip lines. Her eyes weren't full of life as usual. I knew that she knew, but she didn't give in. A few hours trudged by, but it felt like days. The phone hadn't rung. What were they doing to him? Did they give up?

The TV right in front of me seemed like I was listening to muffled conversations from across the room. I couldn't focus on anything. I kept thinking that he was already gone; all I needed was a phone call to confirm my crying. Mom still had her arm wrapped around me, lightly brushing my shoulder. I wanted to be strong for her, but somehow those sneaky tears kept dripping from my eyes for hours. She knew I was sad, and I knew she was too, but we couldn't look each other in the eye. If we did, it would confirm all our fears, and that was too real.

Finally, the phone rang. Mom ran to pick it up.

"Hello? Is he ok? What happened? Oh. Oh no. I can't believe this! Okay, take your time... Love you too."

The phone clicked, and her face peered outside the kitchen wall. My heart stopped; I knew she was going to deliver me the news I didn't want to hear.

"Who was that Mom? Is he ok? What happened?" Millions of questions were going through my head.

"That was Grandma. She said that Grandpa had a stroke and collapsed in the kitchen... They tried everything they could, but he was already gone." The words came at me in slow motion, each one slapping me in the face. They stung; I could tell it hurt her to say them.

I stayed collected though. I didn't want to believe the news. I calmly walked myself to the bathroom, shut the door, and locked it behind me. Sitting on the edge of the bathtub with my face in my hands, I wondered if this was all a dream. Everything happened so suddenly. I couldn't be losing him, not so abruptly.

I looked in the mirror and realized that I would never be seeing his face again... That was when the emotions poured out of me. This was not normal crying. I was practically screaming, gasping for air. I couldn't stop. I paced the room while smiting God, asking him why he was yanked from my side.

"Kayla, sweetie. Let me in please!" I could almost feel her motherly instinct through the door to hug me. I didn't want to let her in. I didn't want to be comforted. I just wanted him back. I knew this was going to be too much for me though. I unlocked the door and found Mom standing there with her arms open. I threw myself into her, and she wrapped her arms around me so tightly. We sat on the edge of the tub together. It felt like my tears could fill it to the brim, and then maybe I would have let myself drown my pain in them.

The silence we sat in for the next hour, comforting each other while sitting on the edge, will be something that will always haunt me. In silence, we find the answers. In silence, we find our fears. In silence, we find our strength. I swear he was there in that moment.

While sitting there, all these moments I thought I couldn't recall came flooding back to me. One of my favorites was a Christmas time memory. It began when I was around five years old. He used to take me to this hall in

Austintown where his Italian Club would meet. They would have Santa sitting on a stage with presents all around him. He would hold my small hand; his skin was so rough and callused around my tiny soft fingers while we waited in line. He would always lift me up on Santa's lap, and we would pose for a picture. Santa would hand me a present from the "girls" pile, and clowns would hand you rainbow colored balloons as you walked off the stage. This is one of the earliest memories I have of happiness. I remember smiling at him over the next couple years that we did this. It was one of those moments with him that I treasured. I still have the picture of us that year, sitting on my nightstand. I stare at it each morning as I get out of bed.

 I could see him clearly in my head, see every detail of his being, but the rest of my senses were dead. I couldn't smell his Old Spice aftershave or the smell of his freshly combed hair that he used to let me style. I couldn't smell the Marlboro Lights he'd light up so often every day. I couldn't see his big, dark eyes—the ones that swirled like galaxies—looking back at me. The worst though was the loss of his sound.

 I could almost hear him whispering his last goodbye to me. For a second, I forgot what his voice sounded like. I tried to replay moments in my head with him, tried to grasp at his sound once more, but it lingered briefly, and I lost it. It's something I will later come to find that you can't get back, no matter how hard you try.

Just then, I heard the front door open, and Grandma and Dad came walking up the steps.

Everyone had stuffy noses, blushed faces, and half opened eyes filled with dry tears. Grandma looked at me first and gave me a hug. As her frail body hugged me, it was like she was squeezing all the tears out of me. I didn't know I had so many locked away. By now I thought I would have hit my quota, but they were uncontrollable at this point. Some of her tight black curls caressed my face as I nestled my nose into her shoulder. Dad stood over her shoulder. He saw the tears leaking out of me, grabbed my right hand, and squeezed away the pain.

She whispered into my ear. "He missed his little girl, Kayla."

I looked at her puzzled and said, "You guys have been babysitting Abbey (my baby cousin) all week. What do you mean?"

"No, Kayla. Not Abbey. You were his little girl. He loved you more than anything."

#

Dozens of cars lined up, all going straight to the funeral home. Everyone walked in slowly. You could tell they wanted to turn back around and make a run for it. Tears practically poured from everyone's faces. I had never seen so many people hurt and upset over losing someone before. I knew he was a hell of a guy, but I never realized how many people's lives he had touched and affected.

They ushered us in first, the immediate family. We were supposed to say our goodbyes and grieve in private before everyone else arrived. I found myself stuck in the door frame, completely frozen. His casket was about ten feet from me. It was a shiny gray color. Flowers from friends and family were draped above and beside where he was lying. There was something eerily beautiful about him. I kept telling my feet to move forward, but it felt like I was standing in tar. Maybe if I didn't move, I wouldn't have to say goodbye. Maybe if I turned around and walked straight back to the car, it wouldn't be real. The line of family members behind me was forming, and I knew I had to take that first step.

We entered the room, and there he was, lying perfectly in his casket. A black suit draped his body, and his old brittle glasses covered his eyes. He was placed in there so delicately; he almost looked pleasant like he was content with what had happened to him. For a second, I thought he was going to smile, sit upright, and say this was all a joke. But I didn't laugh, and he didn't move.

I stood a good distance away from him at first. It was creepy that he could lie there so beautifully and perfect, yet have no life run through his veins. His body was still plump and round. I thought that maybe when you died, they took your organs and everything else inside of you out. He would look different then. But it seemed like everything was still intact. His cheeks were still pudgy; his lips were still full. His color wasn't great for obvious reasons. I wanted to touch him, but I also didn't. For some reason, I couldn't get the sound of Jell-O out of my head. You know when you suck a cube of Jell-O in between your teeth, and it makes that *squish* sound before it hits the back of your throat? I thought his body would make that sound if I touched it, like his flesh would be stuck to his bones like that. So, I didn't.

Grandma insisted that I go say goodbye, but I didn't want that. I couldn't move, or maybe I just didn't want to. If I said those words to him, simply said, "Goodbye grandpa. I love you," it would be too real. That would mean it was over with, and I wasn't ready for that. But she gave me a little nudge forward towards him, and I had to face reality.

I put one foot in front of the other towards the casket; my pulse grew louder in my ears with each inch I crept. I was five feet away from him, but it seemed like miles were between us. He looked a bit scary up close. His eyes were too tightly closed. Even if he wanted to wake up again, I don't think they would move. His lips were an awful fleshy pink color. I could tell that they used the wrong shade of makeup on him. His strands were combed perfectly into place, which was something I didn't see much from him. It looked like they put in a lot of work here. I felt like I was in some weird funky wax museum where I knew it was him, but they strategically messed up a few things to confuse me. My brain knew it was him; it at least registered that, but this all seemed like a big magic trick. I got over my fear and placed my hand on his. Surprisingly, it was smooth. It was like they buffed his skin over. None of his skin was pinched up or represented a dehydrated hand. His dark veins were not present. It was like everything that made him old, all his imperfections, were wiped away.

I tried to get the words out, but my shaky lip kept me from delivering them. Blinded by my tears, I whispered, "I love you," and I quickly escaped towards the restroom. I made it in the stall just in time. The room was spinning, and I let myself fall against the wall and hit the floor. I couldn't handle it; I couldn't catch my breath.

I let the tears fall down my cheeks, tiny daggers stung my heart and skin. I let myself take it all in. This was not a time to look pretty or to be strong. This was a time to say goodbye and let the hurt wash over me. My younger cousins came, banging on the door to check on me, but I hurried them away. I needed to be alone. I needed to let this consume me. After about a half hour of calming myself down, I went back out to surround myself with family.

Some of my close friends showed up to support me. They sat with me and told me how sorry they were for my loss, but I couldn't really pay attention to much else they were saying. They saw the tear stains on my face, but they didn't know how empty and alone I was on the inside. They didn't know that while they were offering distractions to get my mind off it, my mind lost the balance it once held.

My thoughts began to shift. *So, this is what the real world is like.* I had been lied to. My eyes opened a little wider, and I realized that bad things happen to good people. The world was not fair. This was the moment I realized that I wasn't going to be the same me anymore; I still had my beliefs, but now they were mixed in with the pessimistic emotions that his death had caused me. I felt my thoughts and energy change that day, especially when we got back in the car the next morning to go to the cemetery.

The thought of him no longer by my side was heartbreaking, but having to bury his body deep underground, where I could never get to him, was unthinkable. It finally sank in. He wouldn't be sitting in his plush, green recliner anymore, watching old reruns of JAG. He wouldn't be there to go swimming with me in the middle of summer or to play cards with when the rain would ruin our day. He wouldn't be waiting for me to come over from school to ask him questions about my homework. He was taken from me. All of my memories were forced to play a slideshow stuck on repeat. We would no longer be creating any new moments together.

#

I lost him the summer right before high school started, right when my life needed him the most. Being a teenager is never easy, but it didn't help me that I was still grieving when I entered high school. I was always insecure about the way I looked and I lacked confidence in myself ever since I was little. But now depression was sinking in, and it felt like the next four years would be torture.

Once he died, I stopped sleeping. My mind was moving a mile a minute, and it wouldn't shut off. I began to worry about the small stuff, and the feeling of anxiety met my stomach for the first time. I never used to worry. I never used to think bad instances were going to happen, but that was all my mind could focus on.

I stopped eating for about the first three months after his passing. The thought of food made me sick. I was causing myself stomach pain, hoping my real pain would go away. I started not to care about anything anymore. All I wanted to do was sleep and curl up in my bed, where nothing bad could happen to me. Over the course of a month and a half, I lost thirty-five pounds. Clothes hung off me. I became skinnier and received compliments, but that didn't make me feel good. It wasn't what I wanted. I just wanted him back. I knew that not eating wasn't going to change his death, but I didn't care to live my life anymore without him.

My grades started slipping in school, and I started missing class because I didn't "feel well." I isolated myself from my friends and family. I wasn't having fun and didn't care to; I didn't want to create new memories or grow closer to anyone. I stopped talking to my parents about my life. I stopped visiting Grandma for a while, because it was too hard. I closed everyone out of my little bubble. I thought if I opened up to someone, they would be ripped from my side again, and I simply couldn't bear that loss again.

\#

I'm not an unhappy person; I'm just stuck in the personality of one. For over half of my life, I've been depressed. I've lost my energy and my smile. My whole family witnessed it, and I don't know how to transition back into the world I used to know.

I'm pessimistic about my life, about love, and about my family. I still find it hard to talk to my parents. They look at me like I'm some sort of zombie that just goes to school, to work, and then straight to bed. I have so much I could say to them, but I don't. I've sealed myself shut to them and the rest of my family. Yeah, sure. I have my good days where I'll let them in a little and open up to them. But I am still scared to laugh in front of them. What a crime it would be to let them catch a glimpse of my smile.

Even the friends that do witness my once-in-a-while smile see that it's not the same. It doesn't shine as brightly anymore, and it doesn't linger any longer. The frown lines have been permanently etched around my mouth. I don't always frown, but I don't always smile either. My grandfather was the light in my life, the piece in my life that knew true happiness. But now that light is buried deep down inside of me with the suppressed emotions that I only sometimes explore. I still haven't figured out how to piece together that shattered mess of the 14-year-old girl that I used to be.

No one wants to talk about him; I think it still stings to say his name. I still have a hard time going over Grandma's for holidays or even to visit. I start to think about holidays with him, or I look at Grandma and wonder how much time I have left with her. When I lost him, I lost my sense of self and hope. It's like they all got buried together. The grieving process still isn't over. I know that he will always be in my heart; it's just a matter of time of putting all the pieces back together.

A part of me disappeared with him. Have you found me yet?

No, Kayla. I haven't.

…

The search continues.

I had to come see you today. I thought it would get easier over the years to come sit with you, but it has actually gotten harder. The dirt has hardened, and the grass has grown over you. I had my chance to get to you when the dirt had barely settled, and I unfortunately didn't take it. There was a time where I would have crawled in there next to you and said goodbye to it all. Sometimes I regret not doing that. I had to come see you today to tell you my secrets though. I want you to see who I am without you.

Grandpa, if you can hear me, please know this:

Your grave is always surrounded by flowers and small token decorations for the holidays. It has been a little easier to move on these last couple of years. I'm trying to finally leave the grieving stage behind, but every time I come here, I still cry like I did the day you were taken from me. I can't believe it has been sixteen years. I stood here, above you, as a lost teenager, and now I stand here as a lost woman.

My life has been empty without you. The family is still the same old family, but your ghost always haunts us, especially during the holidays. You aren't there to carve the turkey and watch the football games on Thanksgiving. You aren't there to tease me with presents on Christmas Eve, and I definitely miss that you aren't there to take silly pictures of me when I'm looking during my birthday dinners.

STAGES OF BLUE

My life has altered drastically without you. I miss you so much during those times, wishing you weren't grabbed from my side as early as you were. What kills me the most is that you weren't there for some of my special days and won't be there for the ones that come in the future. Grandma always tells me how proud you would be of me. She cried during my graduations, all three of them. I wish you could have been there for my biggest moments. You won't be there when I get married or have kids, but I know I'll talk to them nonstop about you. I love you; I haven't stopped. I just wish I would have had the chance to hug you and tell you that one last time.

I needed to say those things to you. I needed you to hear those words from me, but now I need you to hear and see the hell I got stuck in. The one that I can't seem to redeem myself in. I don't blame you for what happened to me. I could never do that. But sometimes I wonder if I would have still gone through this mess if you hadn't left me so suddenly.

KAYLA JESWALD

When the Monster Took Over

Grandpa, listen...

It happened fifteen years ago... The monster finally consumed me. It preyed on me at my weakest moment. I could feel its teeth sinking in and holding on for dear life. It made sense for it to target me at this point in my life. I had just lost someone I loved. I was grieving; but fifteen years later, the bite marks are still fresh, and the wound is still throbbing. Sure, at times, it loosened its grip and let my scar breathe. It was like it was giving me a glimpse of hope, a moment of inspiration, but just as I'd catch my breath, it would beat it back out of my again.

Though overpowering and overbearing to my life, my monster is invisible. Close friends and family members can see the battle I go through daily; but new friends and acquaintances will probably not see the setbacks of my struggle. To most, it just seems like I've changed, possibly even become boring or sad. But what they don't know is that I've lost myself. Chronic depression, bipolar tendencies, and severe anxiety has taken away my childhood, my teenage years, and has slowly consumed my 20s. It all started the summer before entering high school; you had tragically passed away.

I remember the incident like it was yesterday. Unfortunately, these images are not something that I can shake so easily from my mind. It was August 3, 2003 around 3 a.m. when I got a gut-wrenching feeling that something wasn't right. You knew how close I was to you and Grandma. You both were my second home. You and Grandma lived only five minutes down the street from my house, and I was usually over there every day after school. It was my safe place. There were so many memories that your house encompassed for me.

I used to sit on the couch, with you sitting in your chair, watching Wheel of Fortune, Jeopardy, and old JAG reruns. We'd eat dinner together at the table, have tickle fights on the floor, and play in the swimming pool on those hot summer days. Besides my father, you were someone I truly admired and looked up to as my hero. I saw a lot of myself in you. You were short and husky (which was how I spent most of my adolescence, though I am still short) with a balding hairline and coke bottle glasses. You always loved to make people laugh and were always so giving of others (which are two qualities of yours that I believe I possess).

KAYLA JESWALD

When I abruptly woke in the middle of that night, I knew you needed me. Shortly after, the phone rang, and Grandma stated that you had collapsed on the kitchen floor. My heart instantly sank. We rushed over there, and I remember seeing five or six paramedics rushing anxiously up their front steps to you. It was all a blur after that. Colors blended together; the sirens of the ambulance went on mute. I felt the world stop spinning, just briefly. All I remember was that your body rushed past me to the ambulance as my heartbeat erupted through my ears. I knew you were already gone. Your body was limp, gray, and lifeless when we arrived. You needed a miracle, but I knew that wouldn't happen. The man I loved died alone on the kitchen floor, and I didn't get to say goodbye to him.

As soon as they got to the hospital, they pronounced you dead. Mom sat next to me, stroking my hair, but I couldn't hold it in anymore. I ran to the bathroom and locked myself inside. I remember sitting on the edge of the bathtub, digging my nails into the ends of the tub while clutching so strongly that it hurt my knuckles. The tears poured out instantaneously. Minutes went by as I fell to the ground, screaming. This was my first heartbreak. Mom rushed in, pulled me up off the ground, and wrapped me in her arms. That was the day I knew I would never be the same.

STAGES OF BLUE

The next few weeks inched by slowly. I still cried at night for your loss. I was still mending my broken heart. If only I could have warned myself for the years of heartache I now know would follow.

I started high school that fall. During a time when I should have been vibrant, had fun, and been a kid, I ended up being a waste of four years of my life. The first few months into school, something happened to me. My hair was falling out in chunks, I stopped eating and lost thirty-five pounds in two and a half months, I wasn't sleeping, I became quiet, and I isolated myself from everyone. My parents started to worry about me and had me go to a bunch of different doctors. Endless tests were run, and countless appointments were made, but most of them gave one conclusion: I was experiencing depression.

This was all surreal to me. I had always been a cheerful, talkative child. What was happening to me? Before you died, I was always optimistic about things. I allowed myself to dream, to have hope in things. Now everything was covered in darkness. My hope fizzled out like a firecracker. Pessimistic and dreary thoughts consumed my every waking minute. How do I make this stop?

Mom suggested I talk to a psychiatrist and be put on medication to help. I was scared. I never needed any pills to make me happy or to solve my problems, especially not at fifteen. I thought it was normal to grieve and to miss someone, but apparently if it goes on for a while, it becomes overwhelming.

I saw a psychiatrist and began talking to a therapist. It was unpleasant and uncomfortable to talk to a stranger, but I knew I had to get better. They gave me a 'magic' pill to help ease my pain. After a few weeks, I could feel my body ease a bit, but the lingering dark thoughts never seemed to go away. I kept taking the pills though, hoping eventually things would change...but they never did. I gave up. I stopped taking them and stopped going to therapy. I thought it was something that I could handle on my own.

So, for a few years, I refused help and simply lived with it. I felt myself slowly being pulled into a bottomless mud pit of depression. One day, I woke-up and didn't recognize the girl staring back at me. I lost me. I still haven't found her. I thought I would get better over night with the pills, but here I am still being tossed back and forth like a ping-pong ball to therapists and psychiatrists fourteen years later. The fact that I went cold turkey with nothing for a few years really didn't help my case, but no one called me out on my sadness, so I didn't budge.

STAGES OF BLUE

I craved isolation. I didn't want to be around my parents or friends. I didn't want to go to parties or school dances. I didn't want my boyfriend to touch me or my parents to hug me. Someone else's embrace on my body felt like it was burning my flesh. I hated it. I didn't want to be close to anybody, not after the tragic loss I suffered. Depression followed me all throughout high school. It roamed the lonely hallways with me. It lurked in the dark corners of the building.

I thought I could battle it on my own, but it turns out that it's more powerful than I thought. I started to think that being unhappy was just a part of my personality. Simple things didn't bring any pleasure to my life. I walked around school with a straight face. Smiling felt odd and unfamiliar. I felt myself disappearing. I tried to talk to my friends and boyfriend about it, but they couldn't understand it. I get that; I didn't understand it either, and I still don't.

It's funny and sad to think that one event in my life, losing my grandpa, can trigger this major shift in my personality and life. Even after all these years, the depression still haunts me daily. I've learned to deal with you not being here anymore. I've even learned how to hide my secrets and sadness after all this time, but the depression still envelops my personality and thoughts.

Losing you and a part of me in high school is only one instance of how this disease has altered my life. I do not experience joy like other people do; actually, I do not experience joy at all. Sure, sometimes I smile and laugh, but only for a second and then it all disappears again.

I hold myself back from doing things and finding myself. It feels like all my dreams and ambitions are right in front of me, but a brick wall is standing in my way. Every day is a constant battle to get out of bed and get dressed. My thoughts are never consistent; I battle myself back and forth over easy decisions.

I feel so numb yet so emotional at the same time. I am a walking contradiction. I just feel lost. My mind races a mile a minute. Anxiety attacks remind me that it's all too real. I've been on and off medications throughout the years. Some were a little helpful, and some made me worse, but nothing has fully taken the sadness away.

This past year though, at twenty-eight-years-old, I've finally decided to go seek help again. I put myself back in therapy. I've finally found a psychiatrist that I trust and that listens to me instead of blaming me for what is happening. It's hard to admit that you're not happy and that you need help. I've just had enough. I've lost my younger years to this disease, and I don't want to lose the better years of my life to it. I'm scared to see where things are going to go, but I know I have to track through the mud to get to a better place in my life.

Some people will say that I'm a normal person and that I'm okay, but it's only because I've gotten so good at hiding my illness. I don't want to hide it anymore. It's not something I'm ashamed of, and it's not something that I can control. I want to start living my life as a happier person.

Though depression has beaten me down over the years, I've still kept this thriving ambition inside me to get better and to reach my goals. I know it can take months on end to find a treatment that will work for me, but I have faith in my doctors and in myself to finally feel fulfilled in finding myself again.

Do you understand now? Do you get how much I miss you? Do you see how completely lost I am without you on this Earth? I hope you can still see me from Heaven. I hope, at times, you can even be around me and protect me, but if you do have any real give and take with the man upstairs, can you please make this stop already? I've grieved and have said my goodbyes, so why does this monster still live on? I've tried to kill it numerous times, but it just ends up killing me. I've come to terms that your life is over and that you aren't coming back. But

KAYLA JESWALD

help me find me again. Help me find your little girl that disappeared so long ago.

STAGES OF BLUE

The Right to Panic

I remember this one time my mom and I were taking our golden retriever, Prince, around our neighborhood block one summer. I was maybe seven years old. I had a great purple sparkly bike with neon handles. I liked to ride a little ahead of them to show my independence, I guess. I cut the corner of one of the blocks and was no longer in my mother's sight. An older couple was weeding out front and had their little Pomeranian outside with them. She was a mix of chestnut and hazelnut colors. I remember her running towards me. I thought she was excited, but it turned out to be anger. I pedaled quickly to get away from her. I looked back to make sure she wasn't chasing me anymore, but when I did, I hit a huge bump in the cement. My left handlebar jabbed me right under my rib cage. It knocked the wind out of me. I collapsed on the ground. I couldn't catch my breath, and I could already feel a bruise forming on my small chest.

Prince and Mom were just rounding the corner. She rushed to my side. The older couple took hold of Prince and my precious bike as my mom swept me into her arms and carried me all the way back to the house.

KAYLA JESWALD

\#

When my family doctor first said the word "depression" to me, I thought it was a joke. I'm just a kid. What did I have to be sad about? I was just entering high school; this should be the best time of my life. The haunting feeling of getting the wind kicked out of me came flooding back, but this time, there was no one to pick me up. There was no one to carry me back home.

Our doctor told me that he wanted me to see a psychiatrist in the area for help. A part of me didn't respond to this. *I can handle this on my own.* My grandpa had just died; it was normal to grieve. I didn't see what the big deal was. I didn't want to see a doctor. I didn't want to say the words "I'm sad" aloud to someone, especially not a stranger. What a weird situation. Who ever thought it was a good idea to pour out your problems to a complete stranger? They don't know me, and they certainly wouldn't after a few short visits.

When Mom took me to this new psychiatrist, the sun was just starting to set. His office had late hours. The crisp air of the fall was just arriving. That was my favorite time of the year. I thought maybe this was a good sign. I thought maybe that would mean this visit would be quick. Maybe someone could crack my personality and solve my problems right away so this would be over with. I didn't think that we would still be in the same predicament over a decade later.

I hated small talk, but of course that's what Mom insisted on in the car. We hadn't talked much lately. I hadn't talked much to anyone, and honestly, it felt good not to. We buckled our seat belts and got ready for the twenty-five-minute drive ahead of us.

"So, Kayla, are you nervous?" Her hands clutched the steering wheel as she turned out of the driveway.

"What do I have to be nervous about? I just don't really see the point of this." My arms were crossed against my chest. My eyes were focused over my shoulder as I viewed the world outside of the window.

"You don't think anything is wrong with you?" I could hear a pinch of concern in her voice.

"I mean, I don't know… I think it's just normal to miss someone. I don't understand why I'm being punished for grieving." God, I hated talking about this. I just wanted to crawl back into my bed and disappear.

"You think you're being punished? Really? You think it's okay that you've lost all this weight, stopped sleeping, and completely shut us out?" She looked over at me as we came to a halt at a red light.

"I didn't say it was okay. I just think I'm having a hard time with all of this. I think it will pass."

She reached over and squeezed my shoulder. "Just promise me you'll tell the doctor all this stuff, okay? Let's let him be the decider of all of this." She must really be concerned. Maybe there was something wrong with me.

"Okay, Mom. I will. I promise." Words weren't really expressed the rest of the ride. The radio was on a light hum. I could feel her looking over at me every few minutes. Why was she so worried? It wasn't like I was dying or something.

We pulled into the driveway of the office. The building had white brick and glass windows. It looked nice enough. I told my mom that I would give her a call when I was done. I stepped out of the white Grand Prix.

She gave me a smile of hope as I headed in. "Kayla, are you sure you don't want me to come with you?"

"That's okay, Mom. I think I want to just be alone for this." I took a deep breath as I shut the car door and walked towards the front of the building.

While walking towards the door, I was supposed to press a button to allow the nurses to unlock the door for me, but when I grabbed the handle, it was already unlocked. It was like they were just waiting for me to walk through. *Maybe that's a good sign; maybe I'll get the answers tonight I've been patiently waiting for.*

Green is the color of envy or a signal to press down on the gas pedal of your car; it is the color I would later come to find represents freedom. That was the color that first greeted me on this visit to the doctor's office.

Doctors' offices are usually cold and bland; they're a place where you sit on a hard, uncomfortable chair and flip through dozens of old magazines to pass the time, but this one seemed unlike the rest. Maybe he'd be different than the others.

Warm comfy chairs were placed all over the room. A coffee station was provided to feed your thirst after hours of waiting, and a light buzz of classical music filled my eardrums. If they thought that music was going to ease me mind, they were sadly mistaken. I was going to need something a little stronger than that.

I walked myself up to the nurse's station. A short woman with a tight perm as dark as night sat behind the window. Her eyes met mine immediately. "Hey there. Can I have your name please?"

KAYLA JESWALD

"Kayla. Kayla Jeswald. I'm here to see Dr. Perry."

"Okay, great Kayla. I've got you checked in. I need you to fill out some paperwork for me since this is your first time here. Also, can I have your mom's insurance card so that I can make a copy?" I handed my mom's laminated card over to her. "Thanks, you can have a seat. Just bring those back up to me when you are finished with them."

The waiting room was huge. There were seats positioned in front of the nurse's station in a square formation. There was also a little hallway along the side that led back to another waiting room with the same formation. I decided to sit back there. I didn't want people's judgy eyes on me. I started to fill out the short stack of papers on my clipboard.

Age: **15**

Is this your first visit: **yes (and hopefully the last)**

What is your reason for coming today: **my doctor said I was depressed (but actually I have no idea)**

Please tell me what symptoms you are having: **trouble sleeping (because I keep seeing his dead, lifeless body in my dreams), loss of**

appetite, extreme weight loss, hair loss, and sadness (heartbreak).

The rest was just boring medical stuff, the usual. I walked back up to the window and tapped on the glass. She was on the phone. I mouthed the words "I'm done" to her and handed her my clipboard as she slid the glass aside. She mouthed back for me to have a seat. I moved myself to the section in front of her station.

I positioned myself, coffee in hand, across from the nurse's window, right in front of the doors I entered through. I could see that inside their little cubicle, there was a TV monitor placed above the nurses' heads to see when people were approaching the office. A few patients shuffled towards the door during the first hour I was waiting but realized that it was locked when they latched onto the handle. *The button is right in front of your faces people. Don't you see it glowing?*

The nurses didn't speak to them though or give them direction; they just stared blankly at the monitor, waiting for the patients to slowly figure it out. This wouldn't be the first time they didn't offer much help. People began knocking on the window and making squinting eyes in the dark, trying to find some way to get in. Finally, they would see the button and enter with embarrassment. *If you thought it was hard to get in, just wait until you try to get out.*

I sat there with my fingers tapping and leg anxiously twitching up and down. I was already sick of doctors. I saw my family doctor a handful of times in the last month for checkups and referral appointments. They also recommended a therapist for me to start seeing as well. Besides telling me that I was depressed, I didn't seem to get anymore answers than that. *Don't expect any answers this time either, Kayla. They probably won't tell you a damn thing.*

My parents seem so worried the last few weeks. I've never seen them be so concerned about something with me. They made it seem like what I was going through was life or death. *Am I dying? Is it cancer?* Nobody seemed to have those answers. Crazy death sentences that I had given myself danced around in my head.

The last few weeks have been rough. I couldn't find a belt to hold up the bagginess of my pants. My cheekbones were protruding against my skin; strands of hair filled my hands anytime I touched my head. They tested my thyroid. They sent me to an endocrinologist and to a well-known clinic for tests, but they all seemed stumped. I hope this guy has some answers for me. They promised me he would, that he was the best.

STAGES OF BLUE

Names were called out, none of which sounded remotely like mine. It seemed like I was destined to wait here forever. It had been almost two hours. I sat there, wishing I had brought homework or something to occupy my time and not let me dwell on the situation. I looked around for a magazine to read, but just as I was about to leave my seat and peruse, I saw a woman was trapped in-between the two doors, not knowing how to exit the office. *This looks promising.*

She wasn't the only one having difficulty escaping, but it definitely took her longer than the others. The answer was right in front of her face, a large glowing green button, but somehow it was overlooked by everyone. *I finally had the answers for once, just not for my own problems.*

The woman scurried back and forth between the doors, trying to see if any of them would unlock but no such luck. The first set of doors she exited through were still unlocked; she very easily could have come back inside and asked for help, but she didn't, just like the rest. *I swear these people are like lab rats trapped in an endless maze with no sense of direction.* Finally, the woman looked back at me through the glass, and I directed my finger towards the button right beside her. She looked at me; her face was slightly blushing. You could tell that she felt silly for not seeing the shiny button glowing in her face. She gave me a nod and was on her way. *Lucky.*

I turned back to the selection of magazines. Everything was geared towards older people. I pulled out my phone instead. This was before the days of Facebook, Instagram, and Pinterest. *Dear God, how did we ever get by?* I opened Internet Explorer and typed in the word "depression." The first thing that popped up was an article entitled, "Am I Depressed?" I clicked on it.

Do you feel sad for no reason or aren't sure why? Has all your motivation gone out of the window? Any changes in weight? Lack of interest in activities you once enjoyed? If you answered yes to any of these questions, then you might be suffering from depression. Depression can occur at a young age and can often happen for no reason at all.

As I kept reading the article, things started to click. I did have these symptoms. Yes, I was grieving, but I guess this wasn't a normal part of it. My fingers began to itch the inside pocket of my jeans. My hands were clammy. My fingers started clicking back and forth against my thumb. It was a nervous tic I developed when everything started to change. It soothed me. I didn't want anything to be wrong with me. I don't want anyone to think I'm broken or need to be fixed. The door to the back rooms opened into the waiting room.

After about three hours of waiting, something I learned would be a typical time of waiting in his office, I finally heard my name being called and was taken through another set of doors to wait in a lonely room by myself. A nurse named Shelly came into the room to take my vitals. More small talk followed.

"Hey, Kayla, how are you doing tonight?" She seemed sincere in asking.

"I guess I'm okay."

"Can you roll up your sleeve of your sweatshirt so that I can take your blood pressure please?" She slid the cuff up my left arm and gave it five pumps. Normal. Good. "What has been going on with you Kayla?" Here we go again.

"Well, my family doctor thinks I'm depressed and wanted me to see someone." My feet dangled off the chair I was boosted up on. I didn't look at her when I spoke.

"Was there something that possibly triggered this, or did you just not feel right one day?" Her pen was ready to scribble down my answers.

"My grandpa just recently passed. I thought maybe this was just the grieving process, but I guess not." I began rubbing my fingers again.

My stomach felt like it was sinking in quicksand.

"I'm sorry to hear that, Kayla. That has to be hard for you." She stopped writing and gave me a look of sympathy.

"Thanks." I looked her in the eye when I said it, so she would know I meant it.

"The doctor is a little behind right now, but he should be in shortly, okay?"

"Okay, thank you." She closed my chart and exited the room closing the door behind her.

They told me the doctor would be with me shortly, but we have heard that lie before. I sat there with my phone, trying not to play on the Internet or look up any more horrifying answers. *WebMD was no longer my friend; it was no longer there to comfort me or answer my questions. In reality, it just wanted to feed off scaring the living shit out of me.*

Thirty minutes went by and it seemed like the doctor had forgotten about me. My anxiety seemed to get the best of me at this point. Endless possibilities went through my head of what he was going to tell me.

Then I heard mumbled talking, and someone grabbed my chart out of the holder on the outside of the door. My breathing got heavier as I saw the door handle turn. The panic set in. What was he going to tell me? I trusted this man to make me feel okay, but his month-long waiting list wasn't very reassuring. Do you know how many things go through a paranoid girl's mind in a month? *Maybe he would finally give me the answers I wanted or maybe the answers I didn't want.* I just wanted answers. I needed them. I quickly shot my mom a text to let her know he was finally seeing me. She wasn't too far away.

He walked in and my heart stopped mid-beat. All the things I feared were going to be addressed within the next few minutes.

"Hi Kayla. How are we doing tonight?" He had a white lab coat on that covered down to the knees of his grey slacks. His thick black hair was combed back neatly. His green eyes were piercing when he spoke. His teeth were a little crooked, but his smile made up for that. He shook my hand and had a seat on his stool. He seemed sincere enough. This might work out after all.

"I'm doing okay. Thanks."

"Do you mind if I just do a quick examination to make sure your health is okay?" He reached for his stethoscope draped around his neck.

"Sure, that's fine." I sat up tall in my seat.

He listened to my heartbeat. I took four deep breaths in and out. His fingers lingered around my neck to check my lymph nodes. He had me lay down and pressed on my stomach a few times. "Did any of that hurt?"

I shook my head no.

He grabbed my right hand and helped me sit back up. "Everything seems normal, Kayla. So, what's been going on with you? Your chart says symptoms of depression." He glanced over the chart. His eyes speed-read from left to right.

"Yeah, I guess that's what's going on. My family doctor and my parents seem to have some concerns about me."

"Are you feeling different lately? Can you tell me what you've noticed?" His voice was soft when he spoke. It was nice that someone seemed to want to listen.

"Well, my grandpa passed away last month. I've just been having a hard time processing that I guess. I haven't really been sleeping well. I haven't had much of an appetite. My parents think I'm withdrawing from things and not talking very much. I've also been losing a lot of hair in the shower." It felt kind of refreshing to say these things to someone, but it also felt kind of terrifying. Admitting it made it feel all too real.

"Kayla, I think what you are experiencing is depression, which I feel is normal with your situation. Do you understand what that means?"

I did, and I didn't. "I read a little bit about it, but I guess I don't really understand what's going on." I felt embarrassed for not understanding my own mind and body. I felt ashamed for not being able to control myself.

"Well, sometimes traumatic events can trigger this in people, and sometimes it is a chemical imbalance. I'm glad you came in today, so that we can treat it right away before it gets worse."

Well, that sounded hopeful. I guessed this would be all over soon after all.

"Let me give you some pamphlets on it, so you can better understand what's going on. If you have any questions after you read these, don't hesitate to call the office and speak to me." It was nice to know someone was here if I needed them. He walked out in the hallway to retrieve the information. I guessed that this didn't have to be a scary thing after all. This could be a simple situation; it could all get resolved in the next few months.

He came back with the materials and went over them a little bit with me. "Kayla, do you think you'd like to be on medication to make you feel better? I know this can be a rough thing to experience."

I had never really taken medication long-term for anything before. He could tell I was a little hesitant on it. "Yeah... I suppose we could try something, right?" What harm could it do?

"I am going to put you on 150 mg of Wellbutrin. A lot of my patients react really well to this, and you shouldn't notice too many side effects, but if you do or it makes you feel worse, you call back here right away."

I nodded. He wrote out the script and placed it in my hand. My mind began drifting a bit as to what it all meant. He asked me if I was seeing a therapist. I told him that I had an appointment set up with one. He seemed pleased about that. I guess medication didn't always do the trick; I needed to deal with my feelings as well.

"I want to see you back in two weeks, Kayla. I want to make sure this is going to work for you." He shook my hand, gave me a pat on the back, and sent me out to schedule another appointment.

"You take care of yourself, okay?"

"Yes, thank you." He gave me a smile before the door closed on me out in the waiting room. I set up my appointment two weeks out.

The nurse handed me a reminder card, and I slipped it into my pocket.

He at least gave me some answers. Other patients left with scripts in hand and peace of mind. I at least had that for now too.

I didn't know this would just be the beginning of it. I didn't know that the medication prescribed wouldn't be the winner. I didn't know that some doctors would become assholes. I had to be the girl with the complexities.

I pushed through the first door and saw the glowing green button calling my name. I slammed my palm against it, and the door opened swiftly to show me the parking lot.

I was free for now. My lungs began to fill again. My breath was returning.

KAYLA JESWALD

My Backwards Beer Goggles

I see through beer goggles,
But I am not drunk,
At least not on alcohol.
I'm drunk on dreariness,
Drunk on darkness,
Drunk on desolation.

I roam the world
With a black veil draped over my eyes.
The grass and sky run together in my eyes,
Gray and blah.
There is no separation of color.
This is what everything looks like to me.

When a beautiful sunset appears
Or a new flower blossoms,
I feel my heart skip a little.
But my mind does not budge.
It quiets my heart, and
The excitement is decimated.

STAGES OF BLUE

I don't stumble or slur my words.
I don't laugh hilariously loud or
Draw attention to myself.
The mind feels nothing,
Does nothing,
Turns to mush.
Nothing makes *him* happy except
Staring at walls for hours on end or
Watching the faucet drip slowly while in the bath.
A blank stare-
That's what I have amounted to.
It doesn't require any energy.
It doesn't ignite any feelings.

I don't get touchy or sleazy or
Try to pick up men.
I don't attract them anyways.
The only thing I attract is
Dismal thoughts and distressed dreams.

I bet these beer goggles are different than
What you had in mind.
But unfortunately far too many of us
Are plagued with covers over our eyes.

KAYLA JESWALD

Covers that hide the light.
Covers that hide the beauty.
Covers that hide the world.

Undisclosed Information

Patient name: Kayla Jeswald
Age: 30 (still in the same predicament)

Prognosis:

Patient presents irritable depression symptoms and intense anxiety symptoms.

They didn't tell me much about depression, just that I had it. Thank God that I'm smart enough to look things up on the computer, read articles and books, and do my own research. I've been screwed over by too many doctors and put on the wrong medication too many times not to be educated about my illness.

Depression is debilitating in itself but having anxiety with it really fucks you up. Yeah, sometimes they share some of the same symptoms, but having a mix of them is some sort of twisted nightmare that I wouldn't wish on my worst enemy. There are moments when I care about everything, every little detail, and then there are moments when I want to run from it all.

WebMD and printed text don't provide all the answers, but they certainly have given me more than my doctors have.

KAYLA JESWALD

What is depression?

Many people have felt sad or depressed at times. Feeling depressed can be a normal reaction to loss, life's struggles, or injured self-esteem.

Sometimes people have feelings of intense sadness, helplessness, and worthlessness. These symptoms can last for many days or weeks and can stop normal functioning. It could be something more than sadness. It could be clinical depression, a treatable medical condition.

Mush

They don't tell you about the extreme memory loss. I think maybe they were scared to. I noticed it almost immediately. You know the sound your fork makes when you slide it into Jell-O or stiff mashed potatoes? I imagine that's what my brain would sound like if you poked it. It was turning into mush. I used to be able to memorize birthdays, phone numbers, addresses, names... I was my mom's rolodex. But now I can't hold onto my age, my cell phone number, or basic names of specials at the diner.

It has been especially hard with school. I knew going back to school would be a challenge, but it seems like every night in class I lose focus in the empty white boards or start to watch the snow fall down through the giant bay window on the back wall of the room. My professors and peers' mouths move like puppets on mute. Their mouths move in eloquent ways, but their words seem to lightly tap my face like fallen snowflakes, but in an instant, they are gone. Nothing sticks.

Sometimes when I am making love to Bryan, who is the new man tangled in my web, I want to call him Chris or Jesse. I don't mean to, and I know that it is him, but my mind seems to blur the lines of my past and what's currently going on. I have memories of time spent with different lovers, but sometimes I can't recall who I shared those certain moments with. I'll see something when we are walking through the mall and ask Bryan about it. He looks at me like I'm crazy. I guess it wasn't him I created those memories with. My brain has no clue which man it was, which is awful, because there haven't been many.

I can have a full-blown conversation about my day with my mother or my friends in class, and five minutes later, I have no idea what we just discussed. I live with constant déjà vu. It feels like I am stuck in a fog. It feels like someone has their finger shifting between play and rewind on the controller of my mind. I am stuck in that awkward space before you fall asleep. Your body is lifeless, but you can hear what's going on around you. I hate that feeling.

My calendar on my phone has become a go-to lifesaver. I write in all my appointments, shifts at work, and socializing times in there. I would probably go crazy if I didn't. If I have more than one thing going on in a day, my mind begins to wind up like a tornado. I have to get it down and out of my head. I started to carry a small notebook in my purse to jot down anything that consumes my mind. *Don't forget this. I can't forget this.* I also have a daily organizer placed on my desk to look at each morning. I like to look at what I have going on for the week. It helps me breathe. It helps keep my mind intact. They're such simple necessities, but my mind would be a shit-show without them.

Sometimes I wake up from a shitty night's sleep and can't seem to figure out if my dreams were real or not. Even the ghosts of my nightmares seem to haunt me in real life. I feel like by the time I'm thirty, half of my brain will be like the mush I mentioned before.

Yesterday at work, I couldn't even think of what parsley was called while garnishing a plate of food. It is something I have been familiar with my last twelve years at the diner. It feels like Alzheimer's is already setting in.

That sounds horrible to say, and I wish things weren't like that. I already have a constant fear now that I won't be able to remember anything anymore in due time. I already have a hard time deciphering dreams from reality. What if I forget Bryan? What if my memories are slowly wiped away?

I mean, let's face it. I'm already losing myself.

KAYLA JESWALD

Lack of Sleep (Pattern)

The nights are the hardest. I'm exhausted all day, but when the lights go off and the darkness consumes me, my mind becomes wired. The anxiety stretches from its slumber and rises like an angry beast inside me. Three shots of espresso and bolts of lightning feel like they are coursing through my veins. My body shakes involuntarily. I try to crawl under the covers and pretend Bryan's arms are around me, but even the thought of his hug cannot calm my body.

I basically haven't had a good night's sleep since this all started fifteen years ago. I seem to need the opposite of what everyone else does. My body wants to stay in bed all day. The aches and pains even linger with me when my body has shut down. They tell you that a "normal" person needs a solid seven to eight hours of sleep a night. They should know by now that I am nowhere close to normal.

I usually only need three to four hours of sleep to function, but I'm lucky if I get that. If I ever get more than six hours (which usually only happens if I'm hopped up on Zzzquil), I am totally screwed. My brain has its own bedtime, which is usually around 1:30 in the morning on a good day. Usually at around eleven or so, I get a strange energy spurt, and the thoughts begin to dance in every direction in my mind.

They didn't warn me that I would never be able to be comfortable again. It's like having a crick in your neck that you can't seem to rub out. I was always a sound sleeper, even as a kid. I could have slept through a heavy metal concert if you'd let me. But now I can hear my neighbors three blocks over, snoring in their beds.

Over the years, I've learned to live with this. I have tried almost every sleeping pill in the book, and nothing has worked. In fact, I had the opposite reaction to almost everything I was on. A few years back, they had me try every type of sleeping pill they could find. This went on for over six months. Every two or three weeks, a new pill was meeting my system, and every couple of weeks, we would come to find that my body didn't like them very much.

There was one that actually put me to sleep, but I woke up with a splitting migraine. I had never suffered from one before. I asked my dad to shut my door, so that I could be in complete darkness. Breathing was a hassle. Every time my body moved even a centimeter, it felt like a hammer was cracking into my skull. I couldn't move. I wanted to cry, but it hurt for me to even let the tears out. That was the day of my best friend's 18th birthday party, and I missed it. I stayed in bed the whole day, clutching my eyes shut and praying it would dissipate. I would never be taking that again.

Ambien was the worst though. It is child's play for me. Half of a pill would knock a normal person out, but not me. I took two whole pills one night, and I felt like I just guzzled two large pots of coffee... Never again will I take that shit.

I was bouncing through the roof that night. I couldn't get to bed, so I ended up playing on my computer before eventually falling asleep about four hours later. Little did I know, the best was yet to come. When I woke up the next morning, I was missing $110 from my bank account and had an e-mail confirmation that I had just purchased two tickets to go see Carrie Underwood in concert in a completely different state. Yeah, so my mom told me I wasn't allowed to take that again unless I gave her my cell phone and laptop before bed. I told my doctor about what happened, and then I asked him to put my on a horse tranquilizer as a joke. He didn't laugh. He bluntly said no.

I would rather live like this. I'd rather be sleepy, groggy, and stuck in the fog than get the horrible side effects of the sleep medications. I'd much rather deal with that on its own than

STAGES OF BLUE

become another version of myself that I didn't recognize. If someone could just punch me in the face and let me get a solid REM cycle in, that would be great.

KAYLA JESWALD

A Low Blow to Doubt

The self-doubt I experienced at first was confused for the doubt that many teenage girls go through. I thought it was typical to be young and feel like I'm not good enough. As I got older though, the doubt continued, and I became numb to everything. Every relationship I've ever had in my life, I blamed myself for how things turned out. It hasn't been until lately that I've realized there are some real assholes and negative people out there that should take responsibility for their own doings. Like Jesse. He knew he was being a dick. He knew about my depression, but he still let me blame myself for everything he was doing wrong.

In fact, most guys I dated did. I made sure to give them the warning speech. "Listen... Here's what you are getting yourself into..." And I made sure to tell them about my illness, about how I would be acting, how it wouldn't be their fault, and how they would need to be supportive. Each one went along with it. Maybe they thought they could handle it, but they were always wrong. It even ate away at Bryan at times.

STAGES OF BLUE

I hadn't been feeling the same way lately though. Maybe it's because the negativity is gone in my life, or maybe I've just come to realize that I am not worthless. I remember the day it used to follow me like a shadow though. I remember the days of asking God to just let a bus hit me and put me out of my misery. It would be like that amazing scene in *Mean Girls* when Regina George gets his by a bus, except there would be no back brace for me. It would all just come to an end.

It has been almost four years since I left Jesse, and I think that has a lot to do with why I am not as bad as I was. Being in unhealthy relationships can make an unstable person fly off the tracks. I don't want to seem heartless; I did care for him, but he liked to dominate. He liked to make me like a puppy sitting in their own piss: helpless, scared, and afraid they were going to get in trouble. He'd tell me how much he loved me, and then he'd bitch about my weight. Last time I checked he didn't have a six-pack going on either. Hell, it looked like he chugged a few of them. The constant chatter about other women in front of me made me feel invisible. I wasn't pretty enough. I wasn't skinny enough, and nothing I did would ever live up to his standards. I didn't want to marry this person. I couldn't. For as much sympathy as he said he had for me and my depression, he sure liked fueling that fire.

KAYLA JESWALD

I actually met Bryan through Jesse. Bryan and I connected instantly. We became good friends. He knew Jesse and I were together, so he never overstepped my boundaries. As time went on though, Bryan started becoming everything Jesse wasn't. He was kind to me. We had meaningful chats unlike Jesse, who always stared blankly at his phone while I talked. Bryan had a wicked sense of humor that always cracked me up. There were moments I didn't feel right talking to Bryan. I almost felt like I was cheating, emotionally anyways. After a few months of blissful texting, I told Bryan we had to stop. I felt like I was crossing a line, especially since feelings were blossoming for him.

We didn't speak for almost six months, and I missed him every day. I hoped he would send a text. I would catch myself staring at my phone, waiting for it to light up with his messages, but it never did. Two weeks before Jesse and I broke up, I texted him. My heart and stomach sank as the message was sending. *What if he didn't want to talk to me again? Did I blow my chance already?* Thankfully, he responded like nothing had happened between us. We finally met up face-to-face a few weeks later for drinks. I told him about me calling off the wedding and leaving Jesse. He asked if he was the reason why. I told him he partly was.

I liked him a lot. I left Jesse because he was pushing me to get married and have kids. Everything was mapped out, and my uterus had a deadline. I didn't want those things though, not right now anyways. I lost myself in whatever Jesse wanted. What did I want? I wanted Bryan, just not now. I didn't want to jump into something right away. I wanted to figure out who I am and what I wanted. I told Bryan this, and he totally agreed. Friendship for now. Time to crack the identity crisis.

I have always struggled to find my identity. It has been a persistent problem since I was a child. I used to sit next to the adults for holidays instead of playing at the kiddy table. I never felt young at heart. I liked talking about my feelings and important things going on, not about whatever little kids talk about.

As I got older, the illness lodged itself so far into my brain that I lost who I was and who I was supposed to become. I didn't know what to do besides to just go with it. The illness is who I was becoming. It seemed like I didn't have a choice. I never had a chance to process things. I have always been so quick to throw myself into new things or onto new people that I never sat back and asked, "Well, who exactly is this Kayla Jeswald girl?" It is still an unsolved mystery, but I'm starting to find some clues.

KAYLA JESWALD

Brain on Fire

It's not that I'm full of dark thoughts. Believe me, I have had some bad thoughts that have even scared the shit out of me, but that's not the only thing that lurks inside of me. There were moments while driving that I wished another car would collide with mine and take my life. There were moments on the highway, while going to school, that I wanted to slam into a back of a semi while dreaming to be decapitated. I thought about swallowing a handful of my antidepressants or sleeping pills just to see if I'd ever wake up.

You also hear about the people on the news who do something insane because of their mental illness. I knew mine wasn't that bad, but what if one day I snapped? What if I really would harm myself? Worse, what if I would harm someone else, someone I loved? It didn't seem like such a farfetched idea. That terrified me. I would try to close my eyes and shake the thoughts out of me, but it seemed like they were latched onto my brain. All of this has been pumping through my brain for years.

I mean, I guess we should talk about the elephant in the room. The year I entered high school, I started to carry a knife in my back pocket at home. It never cut through my skin, but it would always trace a nice light white line across my wrists.

There were nights that I would carry it into my room or down into the basement and just cry uncontrollably while it traced my skin. The icy blade felt comforting against my warm rough skin.

I picked a steak knife from our kitchen drawer once. It wasn't sharp enough to cut straight through, but I knew if I wanted to, it would get the job done. Thoughts of ending my life have crossed my mind more than I'm willing to admit. At the age of fifteen, I thought about ending it all. I couldn't do it though. I always saw my grandpa's face when it got really bad, and I knew that calling it quits is something he wouldn't want for me.

The bad thoughts stopped for a while until about seven years ago when I was with Chris. The thought of marrying him, someone who I clearly knew was not the one for me, made me miserable. There were days I would have to pull into an old abandoned church parking lot near my house and just cry. I don't mean the type of held in crying you do in the movie theater. I was screaming, gasping for air, with hot tears burning my cheeks. Traffic passed a few feet from me, but no one seemed to notice the drama taking place in my car. Those uncontrollable cries seemed to be a pattern with me.

The same cries haunted me when Jesse came into my life. I remember collapsing in my hallway. Sitting with my back against the pillar, I grabbed bits of carpet under my fingers. I remember calling my best friend, Addy, to come stop me from doing something stupid. She had never seen me like that before. She had never heard me admit that I wanted a random car to hit me and make it all stop.

STAGES OF BLUE

Well I'm Not PMS-ing

Being irritable, in my experience, can take many forms... Sometimes too many forms. I used to have patience with people. I used to be able to tell if I was truly irritated with someone or if my depression was getting the best of me. It's too hard to tell anymore. I walk away from situations with people if things get heated. I need time to calm down and act rationally about the situation.

I feel bad for my parents, especially my mom. She gets the worst of it from me. Granted, she does have OCD and asks me the same frickin' question eighteen times a day. I try to be calm with her, but it's never easy. She repeats herself all day long, telling me the same things like a broken record. I always end up snapping. Sometimes I ignore her; sometimes I mumble things under my breath. I hate this. We were just starting to rebuild a relationship between us the last few months. I pushed her away all of these years. Her hugs burned my skin. Now, I was finally letting her in, but sometimes this demon got the best of me.

My poor mother. I wish I could make it stop. I wish I could make my words soft instead of always punching her in the face with them.

She understands though. She has gone through this herself at one point. She knows the daily battle I struggle with. It's funny how we hurt the ones close to us, isn't it? Even when they totally understand us better than anyone else.

I feel bad for the guys I've obliterated in my path. Poor things. They didn't stand a chance. I tried to warn each of them about what they were getting into. Depression doesn't come with a guidebook, and it's very hard to describe to people who haven't gone through it. I tried my best though. I told them about how crazy I can be. How heartless, cold, and numb I can be, but they still chose to love me. If only I had chosen the same thing... I walked away each time without shedding a tear. I crushed them. I stomped on their hopes of building a future with someone they cared about. I made them lose their hope of what love is.

They would always ask me what's wrong when I would get quiet. I didn't want to tell them. I'd run. It's not that I can't express my emotions to someone, but I needed a moment to ask myself, "Well, are they being a dumb-ass or is my depression making me feel this way?" The first two times, it was my depression; the last two guys though were just being dumb-asses.

STAGES OF BLUE

Unfortunate Events

I never had a lot of time for really being a kid, even in high school. I started working at the diner when I turned sixteen. That took a lot of time from my weekends with my friends. In reality, it became my excuse when I didn't want to be with anyone. I'd tell them I'd have to work, and I'd miss another chance to make memories. I missed the bonfires, the late-night burger eating at Sheetz, and the sneaking of alcohol into a friend's house. I do regret it sometimes now. I feel like I never really got to enjoy my younger days; but a part of me didn't want to. It all seemed childish to me. I wasn't better than anyone else. I never felt that way, but it didn't seem exciting to me.

 I was always an active kid: a dancer, a softball player... I was just always outside playing. When grandpa died, I stopped everything. My flexible joints began to fuse together. My beautifully turned ballet hips lost their rotation. Bursitis set in at a young age. I was losing my range of motion.

 It was hard to get out of bed. It was hard to make decisions. My friends started growing in different directions than me, and frankly, I didn't care. I craved isolation; I still do. I never knew silence could be such a peaceful sound. The quiet can be a scary place though. Your thoughts take voice and become loud in your head. When you are sad or unhappy, you definitely don't want those types of thoughts creeping in. I couldn't even enjoy being alone. The walls began to close in on me. My mind was now getting a taste of claustrophobia.

My bedroom, my haven, was now a room that seemed to hate me. I wanted to throw everything away in my sight. I couldn't even sit on my bed without losing focus. The books that lined my bookshelf were now reminders that my brain couldn't process their words. The cursor blinking on my laptop of a blank page in Microsoft Word reminded me that the words would not come.

Somehow through all of this, I managed to get myself a boyfriend when I was a sophomore in high school. His name was Travis. We met in homeroom freshmen year. We were in marching band together and began to share a bus seat when we travelled for away games. One day, he asked me to be his girlfriend.

I don't know if it was the depression or just me not being ready, but I never wanted to have sex with him. It was never about that. We liked each other. We were kids. I was attracted to him, don't get me wrong. Other things happened underneath the blankets while we would lie on the couch, but it never got to that point. Not in the four years we dated. Sex was never something that crossed my mind. It wasn't even an option that I thought about.

I had never been boy crazy though. I was never one of those little girls giggling or whispering to friends about the cute boy I had a crush on in class. I didn't care. Looks were shallow anyways. I wanted something deeper. Someone who could make me laugh and have long talks with me. I never experienced puppy love. I never drooled over NSYNC or Backstreet Boys posters taped to my wall. I haven't and never will drool over Channing Tatum in Magic Mike. I wanted more than that.

I didn't have much of a sex drive for a supposed hormonal teen. I think all the Wellbutrin and mood stabilizers were killing it. Travis never minded though. He was supportive of me getting better. He was also a nerd and always had his head in a book. He didn't want to knock me up. He had goals. He wanted to be successful and go to college, not be a baby daddy at sixteen-years-old. He never pressured me about it. I think he was just trying to be nice, but in reality, maybe he just didn't want to lose his virginity to the sad girl at school.

It has been different with Bryan the past few years. I crave sex and attention more than anything. I don't know if it's because of all the passion that is there or the fact that he actually engages in foreplay with me instead of jumping on top of me, but I've never experienced it before. I lost my virginity when I was twenty-one, and it was not how I imagined. Apparently, my vagina decided to go into hibernation for about five years. She didn't feel much down there. I know that was probably the medication too. They can ruin those kinds of things, but for a young woman, sex became something I hated.

I thought that was how it was going to be. That I would just go through the motions, act pleased, and that was that. I think when I started to speak up the last two years to my doctors about side effects and concerns that I was having, everything started to get a little better. It's embarrassing to talk to your doctor about your sex problems, especially when the medication is helping everything else. But sex is important too, right?

Don't get me wrong. I wanted my motivation back for other activities as well, but damn, what I wouldn't give to have an orgasm with the man I love. The last few pills really killed my swag. You could shove a hammer up there, and I wouldn't even notice. She was drier than the Sahara. I told my doctor that I needed this to change. I am an affectionate person, and now I cannot perform the one act that shows that to Bryan. She put me on a new pill immediately. I woke up and at least had an urge for him to touch me. That counts for something, I guess.

KAYLA JESWALD

Cellulite: My Life Story Told in Braille

Pros: I lost thirty-five pounds in two months from lack of eating.

Cons: I now have cellulite and stretch marks from the rapid loss, none of my clothes fit, and I fucked up my metabolism.

Apparently, puberty got the call to attack my body right when I decided to stop doing all of my physical activities. I gained about forty pounds at this point, which was something my small frame was not used to handling. Travis's friends called me fat behind my back. Freshmen year, we took a band trip to Chicago. I roomed with my three best friends: Angie, Carissa, and Adrienne. We stayed up late, taking funny pictures with each other. Adrienne snapped a picture of me while putting my makeup on. My ass looked like it ate itself. I was turning into a mini J. Lo but not in a sexy way. That picture still makes me want to vomit.

    I had always been a skinny kid. I didn't know what to do with all this extra weight...

Thankfully, I didn't have to struggle for long with it.

Right after my grandpa died, I lost my appetite completely. The thought of food made me sick. I wanted to vomit every time I tried to swallow one of those gross school lunches. Within two months, a part of me was gone. My pants sagged, and everything felt loose. But every time I looked in the mirror, I still saw that sad, overweight girl. I had lost the weight, but I couldn't lose her.

I was thirty-five pounds lighter, but the pain still weighed me down. It felt like a brick was tied to my ankles, and someone threw me out to sea to sink into the abyss. My hair started falling out in bunches. My skin was lightly breaking out in pimples. I didn't know what was happening to me. Stretch marks and cellulite began to take over my hips, thighs, and stomach. I guess when you lose weight rapidly, those things can happen.

Now when my reflection glares back at me, I still see the overweight girl from high school staring back at me. The dimples and stretch marks are still in the same places. My past will always haunt me sometimes. Even after all those years, those markings still cover my body to remind me of the struggle it went through.

KAYLA JESWALD

Banged Up

I've always bruised very easily, even as a kid. The doctors always said I was probably anemic. Black and blue splotches show up too easily on my frail white skin. I'm used to these markings, and I know their pain.

But this pain was different. There were days I would wake up and feel like a truck had hit me. It looked like someone took their anger out on me with a baseball bat.

My legs would throb from my thighs down to my ankles. My arms felt like I scooped a hundred scoops of solid ice-cream. There were pains in my neck that I couldn't seem to crack. I felt like I was living in an eighty-year-old's body. Walking became a chore. I felt like I was dragging a big sack of potatoes around. My bones became heavy. I knew this wasn't normal.

I remember getting my mom to call me off school one time because my upper back felt like someone took a knife and stabbed each vertebra. I thought depression was supposed to just make you sad. Wasn't it bad enough that I was in a mental war with myself? Now I have to feel like the shit got kicked out of me too? How was this fair?

STAGES OF BLUE

    The aches and pains stuck around for a while. They really didn't dissipate until this last year or so. I think getting rid of all the dark baggage these last few years with Jesse has really helped heal my body. For once, I can just deal with aches and perks of getting older while not having to blame it on something else.

KAYLA JESWALD

Keep Calm and...

Now this is the one symptom that I still can't wrap my head around. This is the one I still struggle with every day. How does one feel anxious and numb all in the same day? There are days when I cry and cry for hours on end about how numb I feel. How does that make any sense? I don't understand how I feel everything and nothing all at one time. It is the hardest thing to describe to someone.

The only person who seems to understand this is my therapist, Dr. Solstein. Perhaps because she has seen it in other patients, or maybe she has had the shitty luck of experiencing it herself. I'm not sure. I'm just glad she gets me.

Just last week, I was sitting on my bed in my dark room, sobbing into my pillow so no one else could hear. I hate that I don't feel anything. I think sometimes I make myself cry just to make sure that my feelings are still there. Maybe that's how I've landed in the place I am today. Maybe that's how I walked away from two men that I supposedly "loved" and wanted to marry.

Maybe they are right about me. Maybe I am just a cold-hearted bitch. I always feel like I'm caught in my own head. Nothing about me makes sense to me, so why would it to anyone else? I like to think I'm a kind person, a romantic person, and someone who gives until it hurts; but then one day, I can wake up, say "I don't want this anymore," and completely walk away from a situation without shedding a tear. Is this the depression? Or am I just inhuman?

Lately, the anxiety aspect of this has been hitting me hard. I was a nervous child. I used to keep myself up at night, worrying about things, but I haven't done that in years. Honestly, I don't care enough about anything in my life right now to waste that kind of time worrying. If something happens, it happens. For some reason though, I am experiencing full blown anxiety attacks days on end. Once again, how do I feel nothing, but I also worry about everything all in one thought? Someone please solve this puzzle for me before I'm completely gone.

KAYLA JESWALD

The Disappearing Act

I was going on fifteen-years-old when I first disappeared.

First Therapy appointment, age 15

Her waiting room was unlike any other that I had been in before. Two leather couches were placed against the walls, one along the back and one along the side; dusty rose-colored carpeting met my shoes. There were two wooden end tables that had small white lamps sitting on them. A neon pink clipboard had my name, *Kayla Jeswald,* scribbled across the top. I was to tell her about myself and fill in basic information before our session.

I heard mumbled talking coming from the next room. She had a patient. I hoped there would be no one sitting out here when I was in there. I didn't want to be heard. My hands were clammy as I filled in the sheet. I didn't need to be here. I didn't need to talk to anyone. I was fine.

Why were my mom and dad even paying for this? Why would you pay someone to listen to you? It seemed pointless to me. Even if I did have some issues right now, why would I want to tell them to a stranger?

I hoped she wouldn't ask me about my grandpa. It would all fall apart from the start if she did. Dr. Perry said she was good though and said she would be helpful. I liked her last name though: *Solstein*. Something about it just sounded pleasant.

I sat with the clipboard on my lap and waited my turn. Daydreams began to prance around in my head. I wondered what we would talk about it. Once, very quickly, I saw a flash of him lying on the kitchen floor again. I quickly snapped myself out of it. Eyes blinked quickly. These flashes were happening more often; maybe I should tell her that. Maybe I shouldn't.

The sound of footsteps grew louder, and the door in her waiting room flung open. I stood to greet her. She was very tall and lanky. She had sandy brown hair with blonde highlights that sat wispy on her forehead. Small lines etched the outsides of her lips. Her green eyes burned directly into me. That was something very captivating about her, something that felt very friendly and welcoming.

"Hi, you must be Kayla." She shook my hand firmly as I handed her the clipboard with the other.

"Yes, hi. Nice to meet you." I shook back.

KAYLA JESWALD

"Nice to meet you too, Kayla. Make a sharp left there and have a seat in my office." I started walking in. She followed right behind me.

A deep emerald green couch sat perfectly centered against the back wall. Two small wooden bookshelves lined the left side of the room. They were filled with knickknacks and books. She must have traveled a lot. A box of Kleenex sat on an end table on the side of the couch. Hopefully, I wouldn't need those.

She began looking at my chart.

"Let me read this over for a minute so I can better help you today, okay?" She looked at my chart with a charming smile on her face.

"Yeah, sure. Take your time." My hands were folded across my lap. My leg tapped quickly. It was a nervous tick. In that moment, I noticed myself disappearing.

I kept seeing him on the kitchen floor, in his casket, and under a pile of dirt. The thoughts were unbearable sometimes. I hated seeing Grandma cry. I hated seeing her all alone. I always hoped that they would go together. They had been together for over fifty years; it was only fair that they'd depart holding hands in bed. I heard fingers snapping in front of my face.

"Kayla, did you hear my question? Are you okay?" She had a concerned look on her face.

"Oh, I'm sorry. I must have been daydreaming. What did you say?" The daydreaming was getting worse. I kept replaying moments with him and the moment I saw him lying dead on the kitchen floor. It started consuming me. I couldn't pay attention in school. I wasn't active in conversations; I could barely pay attention. I started disappearing and so did my mind.

"I was just wondering how you've been doing since your grandpa died? I think that's what we'll devote today's session to if that's okay with you."

Okay. I hated the thought of talking to a stranger. What was the point? They couldn't bring him back. They couldn't fix my broken heart. They say time heals all wounds, but it has been months, and it still feels like the day he died.

"I guess I've been okay. I don't really feel like I used to. I just miss him." I looked down at my thumbs. They were rubbing together again.

"What do you mean by you don't feel like you used to?" She flipped the page of my chart and was ready to take notes.

"I just don't seem to feel happy or be cheerful. At least, that's what everyone has said."

"So, people have made comments about this?"

Didn't I just say that? "Mainly my parents and some friends, but that's about it. I mean, I guess I've noticed some changes. I've lost some weight, and I'm not sleeping very well. My new doctor told me that I have depression." I shrugged my shoulders.

"You don't think that you do?" She looked up front my chart.

"Well, I mean I guess they are right. I just never thought that was a possibility for me. I never really knew much about it before." I crossed my legs and relaxed against the sofa. I guess talking to her seemed easier than I thought.

"I see Dr. Perry put you on Wellbutrin? Do you think that's helping?" She was scribbling again.

"I mean, it has only been a few weeks, but I guess my sleep has been a little better. I have a little more motivation, but I still feel sad." I crossed my arms across my chest and began rubbing my forearm.

"I think being sad is normal for what you are going through. Plus, antidepressants can take a while to get in your system. Hopefully, you'll notice a change soon." She gave me another charming smile. I liked her. She was sincere in what she was saying. She actively listened to me and didn't make me feel bad or ashamed about what I was saying. Maybe this would work out after all.

We talked about my grandpa the whole hour session. We talked about how I missed him. We talked about the good memories I remember with him and also about the bad moments towards the end, the ones where he got aggressive with me. We used to have tickle fights, but then one day he tightened his grip around my arm and wouldn't let go even when I told him that he was hurting me. Grandma had to step in and release him from me. We also talked about how he kept saying how he wanted to die when they made him carry around an oxygen tank for his bad lungs.

"Well, Kayla, our session is done for today. How do you feel?" She closed my chart and placed it on her desk.

"Honestly, I thought I would hate this, but I really liked talking to someone with an unbiased judgment on things." I was on the edge of the couch.

"I think you made really good progress today. It was nice meeting with you. I think we should continue these sessions, yeah? How about you come back in two weeks?" She began filling out a date card for me.

"Sure, that sounds good." I was actually glad to be going back.

But I knew by the time I would see her in two weeks, another part of me would disappear and be gone. It was already slowly happening.

STAGES OF BLUE

Black Heart

A starless night sky. The color of tar sticking to your shoe. Close your eyes and see the darkness that lives in your nightmares. This is the color of my heart. I wouldn't call it evil. I don't feel like a bad person, but there is a chill that lives inside there. I guess I would maybe describe it as sheets of ice stretched in all directions. Darkness isn't usually the right word to describe what's in someone's heart. Most would think of the organ pumping life into you as vibrant. The color vanished from mine years ago. I barely remember the life that used to live inside of it.

In school, we learn that the heart is the most vital organ in the body. It is in charge of pumping blood through our veins to the organs that need it, so we stay alive. The last time I checked, my heart was pumping sludge through my veins. You could almost trace the darkness on my pale arms. My body wasn't always like this, and my heart wasn't always frozen and bitter. When I was younger, I was considered 'normal.' My heart was fleshy, bloody, and pink. The blood that ran through my veins was like a fine wine. But the day he died, my heart froze over.

From that point on, I didn't let anyone in. I held my parents at arm's length. I didn't want to see Grandma. I didn't want to get close to anyone again, because chances are, they would die like everyone does, and I wouldn't be able to handle it.

People still think I'm caring, still think that I'm giving and kind. I am those things still, but I'm also pessimistic. I don't show emotions, and I detach myself from everything. Thank God I can hide my rotting heart inside me. I hate my heart, so I can only imagine how others would view it.

It wasn't my fault though. I wish people could know that. He left me here alone, and before I knew it, depression and anxiety consumed my whole being. My warm, caring heart melted away, and in its place, a rock-hard piece of coal formed.

My dad sometimes calls me "The Man-Eater," because I break hearts and act like nothing just happened. I can't feel anymore. I just know that I get irritated with people's bullshit, and then I walk away and move onto the next target. I think some people would call it a blessing to not be heartbroken in these types of situations, but what they don't get is that if it's that easy to walk away, then did I ever feel love to begin with? I used to believe that true love existed, and a part of me still does to a certain extent, but I don't think I'm capable of feeling it. I feel infatuation. I feel lustful, but those aren't love.

    I thought medication would help. I thought I would stop being irritated and angry, and I would begin to warm up again, but it still hasn't happened. Maybe I am on the wrong pills. Maybe I can't come back from this. Maybe I never had a heart to begin with.

    I try to close my eyes and forget about the day. I try to wash it away and start over new. But even when I wake up in the morning, it feels like my eyes are still squeezed shut, and the nightmare still hasn't ended.

KAYLA JESWALD

Undisclosed Information Part 2

I used to be anxious when I was a kid. There were nights I would make myself so nervous before a big test at school. I would barely sleep. My mind would race one hundred miles an hour. This kind of tapered off as I grew older. When my doctor told me I was experiencing anxiety symptoms, I had to question him. I didn't feel worried or nervous or anxious about anything. In fact, I barely felt anything. But my body was shaking. My hands trembled all day long. Each morning, I was met with the feeling of a brick sitting on my chest.

I wasn't so much experiencing the mental symptoms but the physical.

STAGES OF BLUE

What is Anxiety?

Anxiety is a normal emotion that everyone feels from time to time.

    Anxiety disorders are different though. They can cause distress that interferes with your ability to lead a normal life. This type of disorder is a serious mental illness. These symptoms can be disabling. With treatment, many people can manage those feelings and get back to a fulfilling life.

KAYLA JESWALD

Barely Breathing

I really didn't think it was possible to feel uneasy and anxious for no reason, but apparently, I was wrong. I've never been one to get too riled up about a situation. I mean, yeah, I'd get nervous the night before a big test at school, but that was when I was young. I had no reason to be worried about anything now.

About two months ago, I woke up one day and felt horrible. I felt like a brick was sitting on my chest. My body was shaking, and my hands were trembling. It felt like my organs were pushing against my skin, trying to escape. I tried the old breathing into a paper bag trick, but that didn't help. I had no idea what was happening to me. My mom drove me to urgent care.

After hours of waiting and numerous routine tests, they told me that what I was experiencing was anxiety. But I didn't have a reason to have anxiety. My stomach didn't feel like I was taking a roller coaster ride. I was just having the physical symptoms; nothing troublesome was running through my mind. The doctor there asked me what I had been taking. I just said my Wellbutrin, 150mg per day.

"Kayla, do you still feel depressed? Have you been on the Wellbutrin long?" she asked.

"I have been taking the Wellbutrin on and off for about twelve years now. I don't feel depressed anymore though. I mean, I notice a difference when I take it, but I don't feel like I need it."

"Did you know Wellbutrin can cause anxiety symptoms in some patients?"

"What? No. I didn't know that." I was furious at this point. Why would my doctors keep prescribing it to me if they knew all of this was going on? Jesus. I've been on this for so long though. Why would this just suddenly start now? None of this made sense.

"I am going to give you a very low dose of Xanax. I want you to take one pill a day for the next ten days. I want you to follow up with your family doctor when this runs out, okay?"

"Yes, thank you. Should I keep taking my Wellbutrin?"

"No. I want you to stop taking that. That may be what's causing everything."

I didn't listen though. You can't just stop taking your meds cold turkey, and I was not about to wean myself off something that has worked all these years.

Later that night, I checked online to learn about Xanax. Apparently, it could become addicting. Great. Just great. Another quick fix for my problems. Let's see what the doctor can do this time.

STAGES OF BLUE

Not a Junkie, Just Desperate

I know that I'm out of shape, but to be out of breath at thirty-years-old really blows. It was never really bad until I had my anxiety attack a few months ago. I don't know why it happened that day. I'm still trying to figure it out. I woke up, and my chest just felt heavy. It felt like everything was built up inside of me, just waiting for me to explode.

It wasn't until I tried taking slow, deep breaths that I realized just how much was piled inside me. My parents got scared that day. I remember going downstairs to do some laundry. When I returned up the stairs, laundry basket in hand, I thought I was going to faint.

My heart started beating really fast against my chest. I got overheated, and my breathing was labored. I kept clutching my fist to my chest. For some reason, putting some pressure on it helped my breathing. I got dizzy and lightheaded. I slowly slumped my body onto the couch cushions.

I've had panic attacks before, but it had been years, and I actually had a reason for them.

There was no reason for this to be happening right now. I just don't get it.

It started getting more intense every day. I couldn't sleep, because it felt like the brick on my chest was going to slide up my throat and choke me mid slumber. There were times where I was just about to fall asleep, and my breathing would stop. I'd wake myself up in a panic. I had run out of the Xanax months ago. I only took the ten prescribed pills they gave me. I tried to get into the new doctor I had lined up, but he had no time to see me.

I ended taking myself to my family doctor's rapid care in his office. They did an EKG. I hated having those sticky squares stuck to my body. They were freezing. Everything came back normal as usual. The physician's assistant asked if I would like another dose of Xanax again. *Yes. Yes, I did. I needed to make this go away.*

I got another ten days' worth, but I couldn't get into the new doctor for four more weeks. I decided to take one every few days, so I could save enough before my appointment. I at least had a short-lived solution until then so I could get by.

STAGES OF BLUE

Drummer on Speed

There are so many ways I could describe the beating in my chest. I've experienced heart palpitations since I was younger, maybe fifteen-years-old. It was never anything major, just small flutters once in a blue moon. The way my heart has been pounding lately though has definitely caught me off guard.

Have you ever felt like your heart was going to claw its way through your chest? I really hope you haven't. It's a terrible feeling. It's bad enough to experience the flutters. It's like a fuse just shorted inside of you, a quick tick of the heart. The horrible thumping inside of me is something I wouldn't wish on anyone.

It feels like my heart is trying to break my breastbone. It flickers lightly, and then a large thump will follow almost like it is trying to plan a sneak attack out of my own body. I never thought I would be clutching at my chest this early in my life.

Putting some pressure on it helps it. Well, I think it helps; maybe it's just my mannerism for putting me at ease. For some reason, when I clutch my fist and lay my fingers against the left side of my chest, I feel better. I feel like I can breathe again. I feel like everything slowed down to its normal pace.

A normal resting heart rate is usually between sixty to a hundred beats per minute. My heart rate was 120 when I was sitting in the doctor's office. Double. Damn. I don't know how to slow down a heart that's stuck in an anxious body. Suggestions would be helpful, please.

STAGES OF BLUE

Nix the Tics

I guess there have always been subtle hints that anxiety would get the best of me. I have seen little mannerisms in myself over the years. They are like little tics or twitches of my body that I can't seem to control.

It all started with the tapping of my foot. I thought it was, because I was trying to keep the beat during high school band or choir. But it has been quite some time since those activities ended for me, and my foot is still going.

A few years later, the tapping worked itself into my leg, especially the right one. The vibrations worked themselves into my thighs. My whole leg was silently burning calories under my desk in college. People always commented on it. Sometimes I would feel a hand on my knee, trying to stop it; most of the time, it would catch me off guard. These little habits grew into me. I hardly noticed when I was doing them anymore. Sometimes, I wonder if my mother's OCD is going to come for me

The last two years or so, it has been all about my fingers. When I am uneasy about something or nervous, tapping my fingers seems to keep me in check. I tap each finger to my thumb from left to right and then backwards. I don't know what it is about that reassures me. My last boyfriend and my mom really seemed to notice it though. They always tell me to stop, or they ask why I keep doing it.

    I don't know that I am. It's like these patterns crept into my mind in the middle of the night and set camp. They are just another part of me now that I need to live with.

STAGES OF BLUE

Living with the Sahara

Remember when you were young and playing on the beach, and somehow some sand worked its way into your mouth? Remember how it made that gritty sound between your teeth? It made you cough when it tickled the back of your throat. That is what a dry mouth feels like to me.

The last few years have been very weird. I thought maybe it was just my allergies acting up or maybe it was the dust collecting in corners of my room, but I couldn't seem to remember what swallowing with ease felt like.

I constantly feel like I have a lump in my throat. I clear my throat so much throughout the day. It especially gets worse at night. That's when my eyes, nose, and throat all start to dry out together.

I drink water as much as I can throughout the day; it doesn't seem to help. My neck and glands feel very tight all of the time. It's a bit ironic that when I try and take my medicine, I sometimes can't get the pill to go down. I've choked before on pills or food; I've choked on water in public and made a complete fool of myself.

KAYLA JESWALD

I have never been to the desert, but I can say that I've experienced it somewhat.

STAGES OF BLUE

Constant Discomfort

Riding the Tower of Terror at Disney is the only way I can describe nausea to you. You get that nervous panic before the ride starts, and then they drop you an inch to scare you. Before you even realize what happened to you, you drop thirteen stories. Your stomach drops, and you can't seem to get in back in the right spot for a few hours. I'm sure you've experienced it to some extent, and I'm sure it's different for everyone.

Nausea has taken many forms for me. I get a stomachache, cramps, or a knot forms in my lower abdomen. Sometimes the knot works its way upward and sits in my throat, making me want to puke. I don't puke. I mean, I have like twice in my life. But it's just not something I need to do. I'd rather feel sick all day. The last few years, the knots have decided to sit upon my ovaries. As if menstruating once a month wasn't enough, now I always have something squeezing my ovaries. A dull ache takes over between my pelvis and hip. I don't know if something is actually wrong or if my body just still hates me.

Saltines and Ginger Ale have always been the recommended prescription for this. They

KAYLA JESWALD

just taste good to me; that's usually why I agree to eat them. I have tried plenty of things to rid my stomach of its illness, but nothing takes as usual. I hate medicines. They don't ever do anything for me, and now I've come to find that my guts hate them too.

STAGES OF BLUE

Disturbance in the System

This is usually one of the worst symptoms for me. I always feel like both of my eyes are pushed together but not quite overlapping. I feel like I see double of everything. I can see clearly, but I can't see clearly. I know what I'm looking at, but everything just seems out of focus. I feel like every day that I wake up, someone dilates my eyes just to mess with me.

It has made the last decade of my life very stressful. It has made it very hard for me to concentrate in school. I can't seem to read Expo markers on a white board very well. I can't seem to hold eye contact with anyone for a long period of time. I need to keep my eyes constantly moving or else I get a headache, or my eyes start to burn. It makes commuting back and forth to school a very hard job. I hate carpooling with classmates. *What if I get in a wreck and something happens?* I would hate myself if that came true.

Being dizzy, suffering from Vertigo from time to time, and being lightheaded is a deadly combination. These don't seem like major things to most, but they are ruining my life on a daily basis. I'm pretty sure if the room would

KAYLA JESWALD

stop spinning, I could have been a better student, worker, and all-around human being. But it hasn't.

STAGES OF BLUE

The Attack on Myself

Anxiety is a monster
That festers itself
Within the dark
Crevices of your mind

You shake
You tremble
Your heart races
You break out into a cold sweat

Your mind races
You're overwhelmed
You're worried
About everything in your life

It takes over your body
Like a virus
It is an attack on yourself
But you don't know how to stop it

You become a damsel in distress
You don't know how to save yourself

KAYLA JESWALD

And nobody else does either
The battle rages on

There is a cure
A magic pill
But you spend all your time
Waiting for a doctor to figure it out

I know my body
Better than anyone else
Listen to me
Hear my cries for help

It takes a few tries to
Get it right
I know when my body
Rejects the pills

It happens quickly
Less than a week
I can tell when it doesn't work
But they will not listen

Give it more time
Let your body adjust

STAGES OF BLUE

But I know it won't
My body never reacts the way it should

It is hard to hold onto hope
To believe that things will get better
But here's to trying to see the light
In this troubling time of darkness

KAYLA JESWALD

A Viewing of Jekyll and Hyde

Session One, age 28

The waiting room was much smaller, darker, and definitely not as nice as Dr. Perry's. I guess that's what you get in the shady part of this town. My insurance no longer covered Dr. Perry and his extravagant coffee machine.

Dr. Rich was recommended by my new insurance company. He was free and not too far from me, so why not? I heard good things about him through a mutual friend, so I figured it couldn't hurt. The month and a half long waiting list was not ideal, but I guess that meant he was wanted, which meant he must be good. The wondrous effects of the Wellbutrin had been wearing down the last few months. The blip effect hit my stomach again, and I was feeling the sadness rush back. All were signs that I desperately needed to see someone immediately.

I visited the Emergency Room twice the last few weeks, because Dr. Rich couldn't get me in any sooner, and I couldn't wait any longer. I was crying at all hours of the day, especially when the darkness fell on me at night. I thought about ending it more than I usually did. I made plans this time. The knife I used to grip so many years ago now seemed like a good option again.

The burgundy plastic chair was annoying the hell out of my ass. I could not get comfortable. My nerves were getting the best of me. My nails were clenched into the under part of the chair as I gripped the seat. My legs were fidgeting. I felt like an addict, waiting for my next fix. It didn't help that the woman next to me brought her five (yes, *five!*) kids with her, and they were running around like idiots.

The waiting room was small enough already. Claustrophobic winds were blowing through my mind. I had already submitted paperwork electronically, so I had nothing to do. His secretary seemed nice though when I checked in. Nice people are always good signs.

The door opened, and a plump older gentleman stood there. He had a creepily pleasant smile etched across his face. His button-down white shirt perfectly fit his gut. He had black coke bottle glasses, and his medium brown hair was full of volume and slicked back on his head. He looked at a chart in his hand. "Kayla?" His eyes sprawled across the tiny room quickly.

"Yes. That's me," I said. I grabbed my purse and headed back to his office.

He turned and shook my hand as we walked to the end of the hall. "It's nice to meet you, Kayla. How are you today? What brings you in?"

We made it into his office, and I sat on a couch across from his big dark wooden desk. His office was trippy. He had a small Bonsai Tree growing in the corner. He had a neon sign with lights displayed in the opposite corner. Lots of different knickknacks from all over were laid out on the shelves. Is this what an acid trip feels like? If so, I wish I could have seen the 70's.

"Well, I've been having some trouble recently, and I'm not sure why. My Wellbutrin is no longer having any effect on me, and I was wondering if you could help with that."

He shook his head yes and said he sure could. "What symptoms are you experiencing exactly?" He was ready to take notes.

"I have had anxiety symptoms, which I've never really experienced before. I don't really feel nervous, but it feels like there is a brick on my chest. I also feel very shaky. My hands have been trembling a lot, which has made it hard for school. I'm a writer. I don't feel too sad. I have crying spells once in a while, and I feel unmotivated at times, but it's mainly the other symptoms that are bothering me." I looked at the ground while I said these things. It has been hard to look people in the eye lately. I think I felt embarrassed that it was all happening again.

"Well, Kayla. Let me ask you a series of questions, so we can get done to the bottom of this."

I shook my head okay.

He then asked a series of questions like if I had planned on hurting myself. I said no even though sometimes the answer was yes. I answered yes to anxiety related questions and some about depression.

"Do you have a nervous feeling in your stomach?" **Yes.**

"Are you dwelling on things?" **Absolutely.**

"Do you have heaviness on your chest?" **All of the time.**

Many more questions followed these, and they all fit what I was feeling.

"Well, Kayla, from what I am hearing and seeing, you seem to be experiencing a lot of anxiety and a little bit of depression. Not to fret though. I think I have just the thing for you." He reached in his drawer and pulled out a bright yellow and green pamphlet. "There is a brand-new medication out for people like you. It should really help with the anxiety, but it also acts as an antidepressant. A lot of my patients are on it, and they barely experience any side effects."

No side effects... What is this miracle pill?

"It's called Rexulti. Do you think you would want to give that a shot?" He looked up from his notepad.

"Yeah, sure. That sounds good."

He handed over a sample pack to me. "I'm going to give you a four week pack to try. It increases each week, so it is a little bit of a slow process. But I want it to get into your system and get you used to it."

Another month of trying to get better. Ugh. I guess it would be worth it though if it worked. Hopefully it would.

"I want to see you back in a month, okay?"

"Yeah, thank you."

"Do you have any questions before you leave?" His eyes were caring.

"No, I don't think so." I usually researched my pills online anyways when I got home. I would figure it out.

"Okay, well go ahead up to the front desk, and I'll see you in a month. If you have any trouble or side effects with it, just call us, okay?"

I shook my head yes.

I headed down the hall and went to the front desk. The nice secretary greeted me again.

"Okay, Kayla. We will see you in one month. You are all set." She handed me an appointment card. I thanked her and headed out to my car.

My mom was looking for a new psychiatrist too. I called her from the car and told her about the good experience I had with him. I think he might be the right fit for me, finally. I told her she should make an appointment to see him.

Session Two, four weeks later

I felt better, but I still didn't feel great. The brick on my chest was still there once in a while. The trembling would meet my fingers every now and then. I figured I would get the chance to talk it out with Dr. Rich at our appointment today. I sat in the same cold burgundy chair in the waiting room. He didn't keep me waiting long. We went down the hallway, and I sat on the couch in his office again. Same routine.

"So, Kayla. How are you feeling?" He sat back in his chair and folded his arms across his chest.

"I feel okay, I guess. I still have some anxiety symptoms, but I guess things have been a little better." Truth was that I didn't care for the medication much, but it has only been a month. Sometimes they could take months to hit the spot, better give it a chance.

"I want to increase the dosage, which could be part of the problem. Why don't we go up one milligram on the Rexulti and see how that goes?" He began writing the prescription before I could answer. He must be getting some kickback for promoting this pill so much. That's all he has talked about during our two sessions together. He put the prescription note in my hand, and I was on my way. Another month to see how things would go. It wasn't the most assuring appointment, but what could we discuss besides what I said?

Two weeks into the new medication, I began getting shakier than usual. My skin became irritated. I wanted to crawl out of it. I couldn't get anything done, and I couldn't sit still. My body was so restless, and I wasn't getting any sleep. I called the nice secretary and asked if I could be put back on the lower dosage. Dr. Rich said it was okay and to still come in two weeks, so we could discuss the next step. I listened as directed.

STAGES OF BLUE

Third and Final Session, another four weeks later

The whole way there, I worked out what I was going to say to him. Dr. Rich, this medication is making me feel crazier than I am. My body feels so uncomfortable and irritated. I feel sad, even more so than before, and I still can't get the brick off my chest. I just needed him to know how I was feeling. I let this man gain my trust, and I needed his help, desperately.

When I walked into the waiting room, the same woman with the five kids was there again... And so were the little monsters. Great. I walked up to the nice secretary and checked myself in. She was nice again; this lady is going for gold over here. I took a seat two chairs down from the woman and waited my turn. My hands were fidgeting again. I always got nervous before meetings with doctors, especially when things weren't working out. Maybe he would give up on me. God knows I have plenty of times before.

The door clicked open, and there he stood. "Kayla?" His eyes scanned over the room. Did he not remember me? I raised my right arm a little to gain his attention. "Ah yes. Come on in." He didn't even wait for me to get up; he was already walking down the hallway. He reached his office before I even made it halfway down the hall.

I closed the door behind me and sat on the couch. Before I even shut the door, something changed in him. His eyes were glassed over. Was this guy drunk?

"Kayla, I don't understand why you aren't listening to me!" He began shouting at me as he walked over to his desk and had a seat. "You are being noncompliant! Don't you trust me?"

I was like a deer caught in headlights.

"What are you talking about? I came to you because I needed help. Of course I trust you! How in the world am I being noncompliant? I've done everything you told me to do!" I could feel the veins bulging in my neck. How could a doctor yell at me? This definitely wasn't good behavior.

"Jessica! I mean Kayla..."

He couldn't even remember my name!

"You are showing severe signs of depression. I thought you came to me because you trusted me. You didn't even give the medicine a chance." He was flipping through my chart.

"Excuse me! I have done everything you've said to do... I've taken my medicine as directed. I–"

STAGES OF BLUE

His words cut sharp when he cut me off. "You have done none of those things. You called my office and complained about the medicine. You aren't doing what I tell you!" His stare was killing me; it was so intense. His eyes were still glazed. I felt like he was looking through me.

"I called your office and asked if I could go on the lower dose. You aren't even letting me explain anything about how I felt. What is going on here?"

"Well, let's just have a look at your chart, shall we? You went to the Emergency Room twice with six weeks, and they administered Xanax, which you claimed did nothing for you. You stopped going to your old psychiatrist, and now you aren't listening to my directions. You obviously have a track record."

Was this guy crazy? He was supposed to be helping me. My eyes began to water. I will not cry. I will not cry in front of this monster and let him reap the joy of that.

"First of all, the Xanax *did not* do anything for me. I called your office to try and meet you sooner, but you had no time for me. Secondly, I left my old psychiatrist, because I did not have a choice. I turned for you to help, and this is how you treat me? I obviously take the medicine and listen obediently. Do you think I don't want to get better after all that I've been through?"

This guy must be delirious. I was on the verge of killing myself before I met him. Of course I would listen and would want to get better. He took a deep breath and calmed himself. Something in his eyes changed himself. I don't think I was the one not taking my medication.

"Kayla, I'm sorry I had to get blunt with you, but I need you to follow my orders."

"Like I said, I am." I could barely get out the words. I couldn't look at him. My palms were sweaty. I could feel my nose about to drip as I looked down at my thighs.

"Look, if the Rexulti is bothering you, why don't you come back in two weeks, and we can talk about it? I have another appointment soon, and I don't have time to discuss this now with you."

You could have if you didn't start screaming at me, jackass. "Fine."

He went to shake my hand as if he cared. I didn't touch it.

"I'll go schedule myself." I still hadn't looked at him. I couldn't tell you the expression he had when I got up and walked out. I walked down the hallway, but I was in a blur. I felt like I was in a bad dream. Why the hell would a doctor conduct himself that way? This is outrageous.

I clicked open the door to the waiting room. A few patients waited in their uncomfortable seats. I hoped they wouldn't have to experience what I just went through. Poor souls. I didn't schedule an appointment. I could hear the secretary asking where I was going as I walked out the door to my car.

As soon as my door shut, the tears began to rain from my eyes. I wasn't ashamed or embarrassed; I was mad. I trusted this dick. He was supposed to help me. I needed him to help me, and now I get treated like a damn idiot who can't follow directions on a pill bottle. Now, I had to start from scratch all over again. There is no way I would go back into that building after that.

I called Brian on my way home. I knew he would comfort me.

"Babe, what's wrong? What happened?" He sounded frantic.

"That lunatic just lost his damn mind on me. He made me feel crazy. I have done everything right. I follow directions! I'm a good person! And he screamed at me! Why does this keep happening to me?" I could barely see through my tears on the drive home.

"What do you mean he screamed at you? Why would he do that?" He sounded upset.

"I don't know, Bri. He wasn't all there today. I think something is wrong with him. He looked drunk or strung out." I tried to wipe away the snot with my sleeve.

"Babe, don't let it get to you. I don't understand why he would say those things, but you did everything right." The inflection in his voice was soft and soothing. "Are you driving right now?"

"Yes." I was almost on my street. I couldn't wait to get home and tell my mom.

"I'm so sorry this happened to you, babe. What are you going to do now?" He knew my anxiety and depression was bad. He saw me at some weak points. I know he didn't want to see that again.

"I guess I have to start all over again." I felt defeated. "Bri, I'm home. I want to talk to my mom. Can you call me later?"

"Yeah, Kayla. Sure. I'm sorry this happened. Stay strong, okay. I love you."

"Thanks, babe. Love you too." I hung up the phone and walked inside. My face was red and burning. It was tear stained, and I could feel snot residue just above my lip.

My mom was sitting on the couch watching TV. "Jesus, Kayla. What happened?" She turned the TV off and looked at me.

"My doctor just went nuts on me. He told me I was noncompliant. He was just screaming for no reason. I was terrified. It was like he was trying to punish me for no reason. He couldn't even get my name right."

"Oh my God. Are you okay? We should report him. That's terrible."

"No, Mom. I don't want to report him." I was leaning against the chair, trying to wipe tears from the corner of my eyes.

"But what if he does this to someone else?"

"Mom, I said my peace. I didn't shake his hand, and I'm not going back. That's enough for me."

I walked around the chair and had a seat. I had to go to work soon. Ugh. I felt like shit.

I then turned into a bad patient. I stopped taking the Rexulti, could turkey, which is probably the worst thing you can do. The next five weeks were hell. It was probably the lowest point I ever got to in my life. I wanted to die everyday.

I guess he was right. I guess I wasn't listening after all.

KAYLA JESWALD

Dissecting Depression: Look at it For What it Really is

I. Out of Control

I didn't see the black ice through all of the fog
Eyes were squinted through the tinted glass
Hands were clutched on the wheel
Face was way too close to the windshield
The moment I hit you, I knew it was over
Car spun out
Silver guard rail banged into the side
Etched into the side of my apple red Cobalt
Head flung forward against the hard wheel
Blood dripping down to my lip
Tasted bitter; I kind of liked it
Spinning out of control
The same way I felt with you
You dug into my side, my brain, my heart
Your black ice froze me over
You were in my blood
Running through my veins

STAGES OF BLUE

A toxic poison I couldn't suck out
You could have left me alone
Could have let me coast along without harm
You're out of control

KAYLA JESWALD

II. What You Really Mean

The Latin translation
Depressio
Means to "press down."
That's exactly what you did.

Pressed down on my esophagus,
Unable to breathe.
Pressed down on my heart,
Unable to feel.

Left footprints on my mind,
Unable to think clearly.
Stomped on my soul,
Unable to be myself.

STAGES OF BLUE

III. Recipe for Disaster

A dash of melancholy
A handful of pessimism
A spoonful of a monstrosity
One cup agony
One pint fragile
One liter of hopelessness
One pound of sadness
Blend together in a mixing bowl
Lick the spoon
Let it consume you
It will eat you from the inside out

KAYLA JESWALD

IV. Out from Hiding

Not quite a masquerade
But not a costume either
I wore you like a mask
A hiding ground for my tears

I went to take you off
Went to untie you from my face
You stuck like glue against my frail skin
I wanted freedom
You wanted me

I learned to live behind you
Learned to mask my emotions
Learned to stop caring about the world
You stole me

There was something poetic about you
Something hauntingly beautiful
Sometimes I didn't mind your shiny jewels
against me
Glue cracked after a few years
Relieved, I was finally free from hiding

STAGES OF BLUE

V. Laying You to Rest

Darkness, age 30, from within my soul
Passed away today from loneliness.
If you care to visit, he'll be buried in my backyard.
Burial will follow at a demented cemetery.
Visitation is not allowed.
For he is gone, and we must cope with that.

Depressio was born in my mind
A solid fourteen years ago.
Such a tragedy to see such a young one go.

He is survived by his rivals:
Happiness,
enlightenment,
flourishing,
lucky,
and unburdened.

Doubt no longer lives on.
He will not be missed.

KAYLA JESWALD

Sunny Disposition

The sun slid into my room through my tattered blackout drapes. I used to rise like the sun: warm, slow, and energetic. I don't rise the same way anymore, though I am still slow moving. I do my best to try and keep the light out, but somehow it always finds its way in just a little bit.

They said I was a very happy kid when I was little. I even heard the term "sunny disposition" being thrown around. You know when you hold a buttercup underneath your chin, and your face lights up like sunshine? I think that's what I must have looked like my first couple of years. I've seen pictures of myself. I have some memories. I remember laughing and smiling, but it feels like it's been forever since that happened.

My face used to glow like the sun, but now it showed darkness like a starless night sky. I was a happy child, full of positivity and hope. But it seems the sunny disposition has been deceptive. I'm now unstable, and the color of the sun now represents the Egyptian dead. Yellow is no longer the positive color of my aura. The yellow is faded, and I've become a coward. My mental activity is through the roof. I should be

STAGES OF BLUE

laid back, but my brain goes a mile a minute. I'm green with envy of the way I used to be. I think that's why the color that represents me is blue. My faded disposition and envy have mixed together.

KAYLA JESWALD

Dancing with Depression: A Five Part Movement

I Hate the Internet

I saw your profile on Match.com one late night while I was lonely and browsing. Your dark crew cut, empty black eyes, and soulless smile caught my interest right away. I had a thing for guys who engulfed the kind of sadness your picture did. I had self-diagnosed myself with nyctophilia. I had always felt darkness lived inside me, but that was more of a figurative thing. I didn't think it would happen. I didn't think that after getting to know you, you would consume my whole being. I lost myself in your huge, overbearing ego.

I thought we would hit it off; I thought your darkness and my light would balance each other out. The scales were tipped in your favor though. The way you said you wanted me, the tone in your voice, meant something more to me. It awoke something animalistic in me that I had never experienced before, but that's not what you meant. You wanted to add me to your collection of souls, and in a way, I wanted you to scoop me up. I thought it would be just what I wanted: to be swaddled in darkness while unable to move or see. I thought I would test the waters, but I ended up drowning instead.

Congratulations on your win, but can you please return me to where I belong? It has been fourteen years. Move on. Find your next victim.

KAYLA JESWALD

I Used to Love the Rain

I saw you sitting there waiting for me
I knew I'd fall for you…
Into you
I was created for you this morning
I blossomed here in the darkness
While the ground cradled me
The rain gave me life
The cloudy starless sky was what I thrived on
Perfect droplets formed my being
Come, drink from me, fall into me
Drown in me.
I'll be your personal puzzle
Only when you put your pieces back together
Can you get out alive
The rain continues to pour
I'll only consume more of you
I don't think you'll survive this storm

STAGES OF BLUE

Common Law, Uncommon Interests

They say that seven years together is known as a common law marriage; if you double that, here we are. I didn't think it would last this long. I think I knew that going into this though. Our first date was epically tragic, but I was mesmerized by you. I always went for the wrong guys. The ones that treat you shitty or make you feel worthless. The ones who think it's okay to get in your head and make you feel crazier than you already are. I should have left you then, but your grip was so tight on my arm.

You dragged me out of the bar. My black heels fumbled on the cement. Your large hand slammed against my skull, and my head and body were shoved into the backseat of your sweet Mustang that you had a sick obsession with. That was the last time anyone saw me; or at least the me they thought they knew.

You didn't let me look back. You didn't give me a chance to speak. You didn't give me a chance to scream or beg for my life. So, here I am. Still stuck with you, so far from home. I tried to make it work for a while; I gave it my best. There was no use though.

We weren't a match; we never were, and we never would be. We always argued. Your temper knows no boundaries. My irritability has no leash. We never see eye to eye. I wonder if that has anything to do with the height difference. You tower over me; now you have two ways to make me feel smaller than I am.

I awoke one morning with a white veil draped across my face. Terrified, I jumped right up and shoved it off. "What the hell is this?"

He was scraping at something in a frying pan on the stove. He looked back at me and smirked, "Good morning, my bride."

My heart sank to my stomach and then fought its way all the way up to my throat. I couldn't breathe. The next four words trickled out slowly and with my breath huffing. "I. Want. A. Divorce."

STAGES OF BLUE

Please Leave Me

I knew it would be a hard process to leave you. You had been in my life almost half as long as I've been alive. You are me, and I am you. Although I want to leave you, I think you'll always linger in the darkness of my soul. Your face is etched like a tattoo across my heart. Even after you're gone, you'll still be the only one laying claim to it. You will still live and breathe in every crevice of my mind. You are so deeply embedded there. I'm afraid the only way to completely lose you would be an old-fashioned lobotomy. I have to leave you though, because I know you won't be the one to walk away first. You are comfortable here, but I don't want you here anymore. You have consumed enough of my life. Your toxins make it harder and harder to breathe. It's time to go.

Please don't think this is an easy 'goodbye' for me. I will miss you. I'll miss your melancholy, your pessimism, and the darkness you gave to my creative ideas. I won't wake up tomorrow and be happy that you're gone, but maybe I will be happy. I haven't smiled and meant it since the day before we met. You've stolen me. You took my laughter, my youth, my everything. I can't give into you anymore. I was raised to be a strong, independent woman. How did I ever get here with you?

KAYLA JESWALD

It's time to go though, my dear. I know it won't be easy, but you'll find someone else to latch onto. Break ups are hard, but they are also where you find yourself. I'm hoping I do soon. Goodbye, my love.

STAGES OF BLUE

Bittersweet Goodbye

I visited your grave today. I even brought you flowers, blue roses, to show you that I still care. It has been almost a year since I laid you to rest, and honestly, I've been okay without you. Better than okay, actually. I've started finding myself after all these years.

My love for writing has returned. I don't cry in my bed late at night. I don't spite God for putting you in my life. I've learned to become thankful for what you did to me. You made me see things in a different light and imprinted on my mind. I am who I am because of your horrible self.

You raised me like I was one of your own. You were overly attentive. Your interest in me never swayed. I was your target for so long, and you never missed once. I admit a part of me was scared to get rid of you completely. You showed me a side of the world that only an unlucky number of people gets to see. I never knew what this Earth was like until I lost you. I'm glad I finally got out from under your grip. You would have consumed the rest of my life. You would have swallowed me whole, and I never would have accomplished my dreams, let alone know what they are.

KAYLA JESWALD

Thank you for growing weaker over the years. For if you hadn't, I wouldn't have escaped. I wouldn't have been able to run away.

I have to go now. The next one is waiting for me in the car. Let's see where he takes me.

STAGES OF BLUE

The Road to Redemption

As you can tell from reading this, I have not had an easy journey. It has been so hard to find decent doctors and the right medications. It seems like my body rejected almost everything I tried. I also had some shitty doctors who did not pay attention to my symptoms or to what I was experiencing. Luckily though, my luck has changed the last two years.

After years of relying on doctors to fix me, I took it upon myself to seek the right fit. I found a doctor not far from me. The only problem was, at the time, it took almost four weeks to get into see her. That was a rough period. I wasn't medicated at the time and really needed her sooner. I went through an awful bought of anxiety and crying fits. I isolated myself from everyone and just wanted to stay in the house. If I did go out, I used every excuse in the book to just get back home. When I finally did get to see her, she talked to me like I was a human and not some lab rat. She understood what I was going through and related me to other patients she had. This was so comforting, especially to know I wasn't crazy or alone.

Some medications worked at first, but within a few weeks, my body started to discard them. I wouldn't react the way I was supposed to. At times, I felt hopeless, and I thought I would be in this endless searching cycle forever. She did find a fit for the time being. I was a little better and was starting to feel like myself.

The only problem was that she was getting so booked that I couldn't see her for over six weeks sometimes. This became problematic because at times, I wasn't doing so well. I hated relying on doctors to fix me, and I knew I couldn't completely take this on myself. My mom suggested that I try her psychiatrist instead. I was leery at first. I thought she would be just like the rest, and I didn't want to get my hopes up.

I finally gave in and went to see her. Immediately, she knew the fix for me within five minutes of talking to me. She hit the nail on the head. Thank God. She upped one of my medications and started me on something new. She had success with this in the past with other patients.

At first, my body did not react well to it. Mainly because it was too high of a dose. I called her, and she lowered it right over the phone. It was so nice to save me a trip and to know she was immediately within my reach. As the sessions went by, she acknowledged that I was having trouble focusing. I always told this to the doctors before, but they shook it off and just said it was a part of my depression. Little did they know, I was suffering with ADHD. She gave me a medicine that day, and I have never felt so clear-minded. I can focus on my work. I can get writing done. I can focus on anything for hours on end. I am so thankful to her for listening to me and addressing my issues.

Like I said, I wish I could have found her sooner. It would have saved me so much time on this painful journey. But I'm also thankful in a way. My depression, though horrid at times, has shaped me into the person I am today. I see the world in a different way. I appreciate the little things more. I am more appreciative of the things I have been blessed with in my life.

After all these years, I finally have found hope and light at the end of my tunnel. She proved to me that not all doctors are the same and redeemed my belief in getting better.

KAYLA JESWALD

About the Author

Kayla Jeswald is a writer based in Youngstown, Ohio. She holds a Master's in Creative Writing from Youngstown State University. She currently teaches composition and is working on her next collection and other publications.

About the Press

Unsolicited Press is a small press in Portland, Oregon. The publisher produces fiction, poetry, and creative nonfiction written by emerging and award-winning authors.

Learn more at unsolicitedpress.com.

www.ingramcontent.com/pod-product-compliance
Lightning Source LLC
Chambersburg PA
CBHW030116100526
44591CB00009B/417